ROME *MADE EASY*

Douglas E. Morris
Author of *Italy Guide*

Open Road Publishing

Open Road Publishing

We offer travel guides to American and foreign locales. Our books tell it like it is, often with an opinionated edge, and our experienced authors always give you all the information you need to have the trip of a lifetime. Write for your free catalog of all our titles.

Open Road Publishing
P.O. Box 284, Cold Spring Harbor, NY 11724
E-mail: Jopenroad@aol.com

Text Copyright©2005 by Douglas E. Morris
ISBN 1-59360-039-9
Library of Congress Control No. 2004118012
–All Rights Reserved–

ABOUT THE AUTHOR

Douglas E. Morris is the author of Open Road Publishing's *Italy Guide, Rome Guide, Tuscany & Umbria Guide*, and now *Rome Made Easy*. After living in Italy for much of his youth, he has decided to return and make it his home, helping to make his guides the most up-to-date and informative available.

TABLE OF CONTENTS

Introduction   7

1. Sights   8
Top Ten Sights   8
Spanish Steps/Via Veneto Area   10
Rome's Centro Storico   18
The Vatican   26
Around the Forum   37
Outside the Center of Rome   52

2. Walks   59
Il Tridente Walk   59
Centro Storico Walk 1   67
Centro Storico Walk 2   73
Centro Storico Walk 3   80

3. Miscellany   85
Accommodations   85
   Rome's Best Hotels   86-87
Airports & Getting Around   89
Other Basic Information   94
Dining & Nightlife   106

Index   111

Maps

Rome Overview   9
Rome Map A   11
Rome Map B   19
Rome Map C   27
Rome Map D   38
Roman Forum & Palatine Hill   45
Walking Tours 1 & 2   60
Walking Tours 3 & 4   74
Rome's Metro   93

ROME *MADE EASY*

INTRODUCTION

Rome is a magical city filled with ancient ruins, winding medieval streets, Renaissance palazzi, superb restaurants, lively nightlife, relaxing cafés, savory wine bars, and unique shopping excursions. Each step you take in Rome will be a walk through history: ancient ruins such as the Colosseum and the Forum, set against the glory of Renaissance churches, all complemented by museums overflowing with stunning relics and incomparable works of art – all of which is surrounded by the vibrant and congenial people of the Eternal City!

Along with the architectural and artistic splendor, Rome is also a city made up of neighborhoods, places where communities fill the piazzas and spill out of cafes, offering visitors a delightful introduction to Roman life. While this book will direct you to the best known sights, it will also transport you to those places off the beaten path where the locals celebrate the joy of Italian living. In the narrow streets of old Rome behind the Piazza Navona or near the Pantheon, perhaps more than in the impressive ruins of antiquity, the true heart of ancient Rome is revealed.

We will guide you to those places that should not be missed, offer a variety of the tastiest eateries, and select scintillating walks through Rome's most memorable neighborhoods. Refer to our detailed maps, follow our comprehensive walking tours, stop at a great place to eat or shop, and let this handy pocket guide make your visit enjoyable, memorable ... and easy.

1. SIGHTS

This little pocket guide, some comfortable walking shoes, and a spirit of adventure are all you need to explore the innumerable piazzas, churches, galleries, parks, and fountains of this unique city. Because there is so much to see and do, the chief difficulty most visitors have in Rome is that even a month's worth of concentrated touring will only scratch the surface. So, if your time is limited, here are Rome's **ten must-see sights**:

Sistine Chapel: Site of Michelangelo's magnificent frescoed ceiling and walls.

Vatican Museums: Egyptian, Greek & Roman artifacts, as well as the best collection of paintings and sculptures anywhere in the world.

St. Peter's: The world's largest cathedral, exquisitely decorated, which includes Michelangelo's masterpiece, La Pieta, as well as many other works.

Castel Sant'Angelo: The fortress that used to protect the Vatican, now houses a wonderful armaments museum. Imperial and Roman Forums & Colosseum - The center of ancient Roman life. A great place for people of all ages to explore.

Capitoline Museum: The second best antiquities museum in Rome, with many fine sculptures and paintings.

Piazza Navona: This lively piazza is filled with fountains, churches, and palazzi as well as delicious cafés and restaurants.

Trevi Fountain: One of the most beautiful fountains in Italy, especially at night, when it is lit up. Truly stunning.

SIGHTS 9

Piazza di Spagna: This piazza contains the magnificent series of steps known as the Spanish Steps. A popular gathering spot for locals and tourists alike. Part of the area known as Il Tridente.

Il Tridente: The trident of streets extending from the Piazza del Popolo (Via Ripetta, Via del Corso, and Via del Babuino) that make up Rome's most popular shopping and entertainment district.

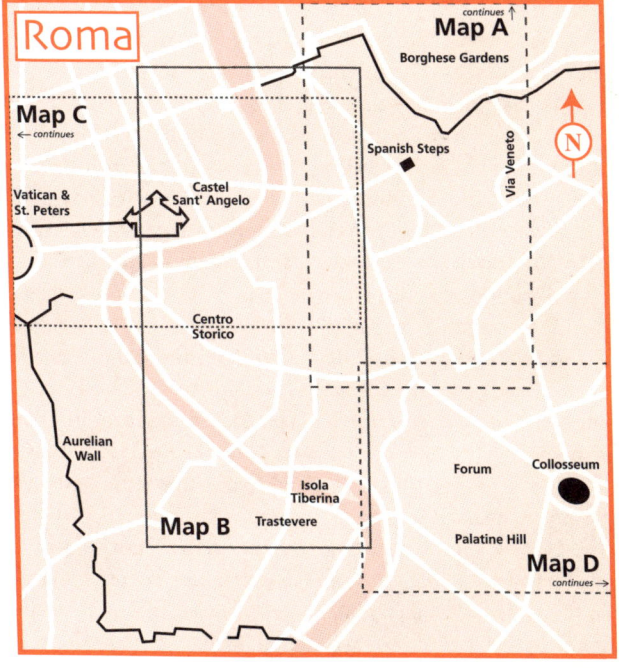

Spanish Steps/Via Veneto Area

The area around the **Spanish Steps** for centuries has been the preferred locale for foreign visitors sojourning in Rome. Some of the luminaries that stayed in this area include: Lord Byron, Keats, Shelley, Mark Twain, and Henry James. One reason for this is that in the 18th and 19th century this piazza was the end of the line for many horse-drawn coaches entering the city. As result, more often than not, travelers would stay in and around this area. Near the western end of the Piazza di Spagna, the Via delle Carrozze (Carriage Road) reminds us of this legacy through its name.

To me, and many other people who have lived in Rome, this neighborhood is the core of this bustling city. Filled with fine shops, excellent restaurants, inviting cafes, antique stores, and memorable sights, the area around the Spanish Steps is the best place to start any visit to Rome.

1. Altar & Mausoleum of Augustus

Piazza Augusto Imperatore. Web: www.roma2000.it/zaugusto.html. Altar open 9:00am-2:00pm. Call to gain access to the mausoleum, Tel. 06/6710-3819. Closed Sundays. Metro-Spagna.

This wonderfully preserved altar was built from 13-9 BCE to celebrate the peace established by Emperor Augustus following his victories in Gaul and Spain. It consists of a simple raised platform enclosed by a four-walled screen with openings at the front and back. Rebuilt and housed in a temporary structure in 1938 by Mussolini to glorify Italy's past, the upper section displays mythical scenes associated with the history of Rome as well as scenes from the consecration ceremonies of the altar itself.

Fragments came to light in 1568 during reconstruction on the Palazzo Fiano in the Campo Marzio. Additional

SIGHTS 11

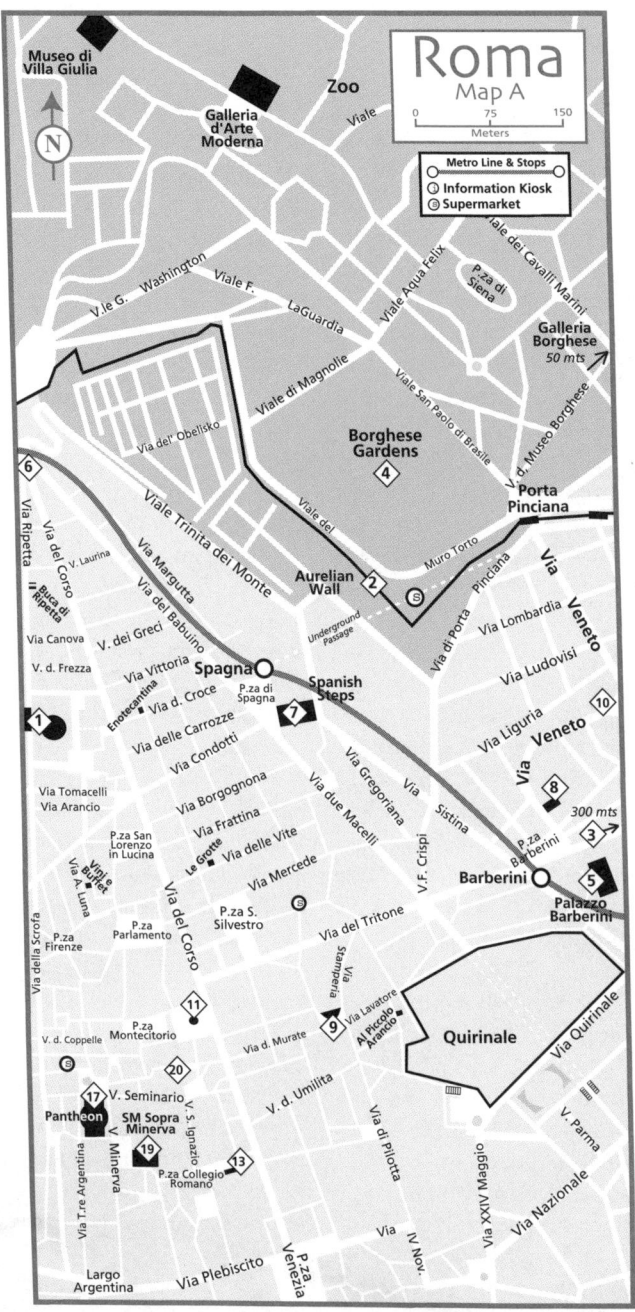

pieces were dug up in the mid-19th and early 20th centuries. Finally in 1938 a professional excavation and reassembly was undertaken; and the altar was moved here.

The mausoleum of Augustus is the circular structure nearby that is overrun with grass and shrubs. It once was topped with a large statue of Augustus, and used to contain a series of intricate passageways where niches of urns filled with funeral ashes could be found. Over the years, it has been used as a fort, a bull-ring, a theater and a concert hall.

2. Aurelian Wall

Built from 272-279 CE, this wall is a testament to the glory of the Roman Empire. Built to protect Rome from an incursion of Germanic tribes, the walls enclosed not only the old city of Rome but also what used to be the farmland which fed it.

Today the walls extend from the Baths of Caracalla in the south to the Piazza del Popolo in the north, from Trastevere and Saint Peter's in the west, and to the University and Stazione Termini in the East. They have a total length of about 12 miles, and consist of concrete rubble encased in brick almost 12 feet thick and 25 feet high. In some places the wall's height is nearly 50 feet. There are 380 square towers interspersed along its length, each are a distance of two arrow shots apart. This ends up being about 100 feet. There were 18 main gates, many of which have been rebuilt to accommodate different defense strategies throughout the ages. Most recently they were adapted for the onslaught of automobile traffic. The ones that are the best preserved with most of their Roman features still intact are the Porta San Sebastiano (near San Giovanni in Laterano), Porta Asinara (next to Porta San Giovanni) and the Porta Toscolana (behind the train station).

3. Baths of Diocletian

Viale delle Terme. Admission €1. Web: www.roma2000.it/zdiocle.html. Hours 9:00am-2:00pm. Holidays until 1:00pm. Closed Mondays. Metro-Repubblica.

These were the most extensive baths of their times in which more than 3,000 bathers could be accommodated simultaneously. Built by Maximilian and Diocletian from 196-306 CE, today the Museo Nazionale delle Terme is located here. If you like ancient sculpture you'll enjoy this collection of classical Greek and Roman works.

Start with the Hall of Masterpieces where you'll find the Pugilist, a bronze work of a seated boxer, and the Discobolus, a partial sculpture of a discus thrower celebrated for its amazing muscle development.

Another inspiring work is the celebrated Dying Gaul and His Wife, a colossal sculpture from Pergamon created in the third century BCE. Then there is the Great Cloister, a perfectly square space surrounded by an arcade of one hundred Doric columns. This is one of the most beautiful architectural spaces in Rome, which is saying something. It is speculated that this space was designed and built by Michelangelo in 1565, which may be the case, but since he was so busy working on many other projects, many experts believe that it is actually the work of one of his pupils, Jacopo del Duca.

4. Borghese Gardens
Metro-Spagna or Flaminio.
The most picturesque park in Rome, complete with serene paths, a lake where you can rent boats, some wonderful museums, lush vegetation, expansive grass fields, Rome's zoo, a large riding ring, and more. If you want an afternoon's respite from the sights of the city, or you're tired of spending time in your hotel room during the siesta hours, escape to these luscious and spacious gardens.

Sundays fill the park with families, couples and groups of people biking, jogging, walking their dogs, playing soccer, strolling or simply relaxing in Rome's largest green space. Small food stands are interspersed in the park offering refreshments and snacks. To get to the gardens either exit the old walls of Rome through the gates at the Piazza del Popolo or at the top of the Via Veneto. Make sure you keep an eye out for those heated Italian couples if you have kids in tow.

Galleria Borghese
Villa Borghese, Piazza dell'Uccelliera 5. Tel. 06/632-8101. Admission €6. Reservations suggested from www.ticketeria.it. Hours 9:00am-9:00pm, until midnight on Saturdays, only until 8:00pm on Sundays. Closed Mondays. Metro-Spagna.
Located in the most picturesque public park in Rome,

and housed in a beautiful villa constructed in the 17th century. The ground floor of this museum contains the sculpture collection, which would be considered without peer if not for the fact that it is located in Rome where there are a number of other superb collections. The sculptures are just the appetizer because the main draw of this museum is the gallery of paintings on the first floor.

Before you abandon the sculptures, take note of the reclining Pauline Borghese, created by Antonio Canova in 1805. She was the sister of Napoleon, and was married off to one of the wealthiest families in the world at the time to ensure peace and prosperity. She looks quite enticing posing half naked on a lounge chair. Another work not to miss is David and the Slingshot by Bernini in 1619 aids to be a self-portrait of the sculptor. Other works by Bernini are spotlighted and intermixed with ancient Roman statuary.

On the first floor there are also many great paintings, especially the Madonna and Child by Bellini, Young Lady with a Unicorn by Raphael, Madonna with Saints by Lotto, and some wonderful works by Caravaggio. A great museum to visit when in Rome.

Museo di Villa Giulia
Piazza di Villa Giulia 9. Tel. 06/332-6571. Admission €5. Tickets: www.ticketeria.it. Hours 9:00am-6:30pm Tues-Fri, Sundays until 8:00pm and Saturdays in the summer open also from 9:00pm-midnight. Closed Mondays. Metro-Flaminio.

Located in the Palazzo di Villa Giulia, built in 1533 by Julius III, and situated amid the Borghese Gardens, this incredible archaeological museum contains 34 rooms of ancient sculptures, sarcophagi, bas-reliefs, and more, mainly focusing on the Etruscan civilization. Items of interest include the statues created in the 5th century BCE of a Centaur, and Man on a Marine Monster; Etruscan clay sculptures of Apollo, Hercules with a Deer, and Goddess with Child; objects from the Necropoli at Cervetri including a terracotta work of Amazons with Horses created in the 6th century BCE and a sarcophagus of a "married couple," a masterpiece of Etruscan sculpture from the 6th century BCE.

5. Palazzo Barberini
Via delle Quattro Fontane, 13. Tel. 06/482-4184. Web: www.galleriaborghese.it. Admission €5. Hours 9:00am-9:00pm Tuesday-Friday, until midnight on Saturdays, until 8:00pm on Sundays. Closed Mondays. Metro-Barberini.

Located just off the Piazza Barberini on the Via Quattro Fontane, this baroque palace was started by Carlo Maderno in 1623 with the help of Borromini and was finished in 1633 by Bernini. One wing of the palace is the Galleria Nazionale d'Arte Antica, which contains many stunning paintings including Marriage of St. Catherine by Sodoma, Portrait of a Lady by Piero di Cossimo, and Rape of the Sabines by Sodoma. A great place to visit in the evenings since it stays open late.

6. Piazza del Popolo
Web: www.roma2000.it/zpopolo.html. Metro-Flaminio.

This impressive piazza is the base of the ascent to the Pincio, a verdant and relaxing area of Rome. Created in 1538 during the Renaissance, today this piazza has been made a pedestrian zone, part of the over 600 acres in Rome that are free of cars.

The 24 meter high Egyptian Obelisk in the center of the piazza arrived from Egypt during the time of Ramses II in the 8th century BCE, and was initially placed in the Circus Maximus. In 1589 it was moved here. The present layout was designed by G. Valadier at the beginning of the 19th century and is decorated with two semi-circles containing flowers and statues. During this re-design the obelisk was placed in a new fountain with the existing sculpted lions.

There are two symmetrical baroque churches at the south end of the piazza flanking the

RESTAURANT TIP

La Buca di Ripetta
Via di Ripetta 36, Tel. 06/321-9391. Nearest Metro: Flaminio.

This small local trattoria serves great Roman cuisine. With its high walls covered with cooking and farming paraphernalia such as enormous bellows, great copper pans, the atmosphere here compliments the great food. When in Rome, you simply must dine here.

intersection of the Via del Corso. These two churches, Santa Maria dei Miracoli (1678) and Santa Maria in Monesanto (1675) both have picturesque cupolas that were begun by C. Rainaldi and finished by Bernini and Carlo Fontana respectively.

7. Piazza di Spagna
Metro-Spagna.

Built in the 17th century, this is one of the most beautiful spots in Rome. Named after the old Spanish Embassy to the Holy See that used to stand on the site, the 137 steps are officially called the Scalinata della Trinita dei Monti, and are named for the church at the top. Even so most people just call them the Spanish Steps. The fountain in the middle of the piazza is known as the Barcaccia and was designed in 1628 by Pietro Bernini in commemoration of the big flood of 1598. To the right is the column of the Immaculate Conception erected in 1865 by Pius IX. This piazza is a favorite gathering spot for Italians of all ages.

8. Santa Maria della Concezione
Via Veneto 27, Tel. 06/ 4871185. Open daily from 7:00am to noon and 4:00pm to 8:00pm. Admission €3. Metro-Barberini

At the bottom of the Via Veneto you will find the infamous Church of Bones. In the crypt of the church there is a macabre arrangement of the bones of over 4,000 skeletons of ancient friars that were exhumed and decoratively placed on the walls. The reason this display exists is that a law was passed many centuries ago stating that no graveyards or burial grounds could exist inside the walls of Rome. Rather than part with the remains of their brothers by re-

---

CAFE WITH A VIEW

Olimpo
Piazza Barberini 23, Tel. 06/4201-0469. Web: www.berninibristol.com. Nearest Metro: Barberini.

At the foot of the Via Veneto, right by the Church of Bones is a wonderful cafe with a view. Situated on the top of the Bernini Bristol hotel, if you are looking for a great place to take a rest and have superb panoramic vistas over the rooftops of Rome, stop in here.

burying them in a cemetery outside the walls, the Cappucin brothers exhumed the fraternal remains and decorated the crypt with them. I guarantee that you'll never see a sight like this anywhere else.

9. Trevi Fountain
Piazza di Trevi. Web: www.roma2000.it/ztrevi.html. Metro-Barberini.

The largest and most impressive of Rome's fountains. It is truly spectacular when it is lit up at night. Commissioned by Pope Clement XII and built by Nicola Salvi in 1762 from a design he borrowed from Bernini, the fountain takes up an entire exterior wall of the Palazzo Poli that was built in 1730. In the central niche is Neptune on his chariot drawn by marine horses preceded by two tritons. In the left niche is the statue representing Abundance, and to the right Health. The four statues up top depict the seasons, and the crest is of the family of Pope Clement XII, Corsini.

There is an ancient custom that guarantees that all who throw a coin into the fountain are destined to return to Rome. So turn your back to the fountain and throw a coin over your left shoulder, with your right hand, into the fountain and fate will carry you back. Please don't try and recreate Anita Ekberg's scene in the film La Dolce Vita when she waded through the fountain to taunt Marcello Mastroiani. It is completely illegal to walk in the Trevi fountain, and the authorities enforce this regulation.

10. Via Veneto
Web: www.roma2000.it/zveneto.html. Metro-Barberini.

Definitely the most famous street in Rome. It used to be the center of all artistic activities as well as the meeting place for the jet set. Though that allure is rather faded today, it is still a great place to stroll and admire the high end hotels, stores, and cafés.

At the bottom of the street is the Piazza Barberini where you'll find the graceful Fontana delle Api (Fountain of the Bees) as well as the Fontana del Tritone, both designed and sculpted by Bernini. Up the Via Veneto a little ways from the Piazza Barberini is the grandiose Palazzo Margherita, built by G. Koch in 1890, which is now the home of the American Embassy. You'll recognize it by the armed guards and the American flag flying out front. At the top of the Via Veneto is the Aurelian Wall, through which you can access the Borghese Gardens.

Rome's Centro Storico

Extending from the Via del Corso to across the Tiber into Trastevere (literally meaning across the Tiber) is Rome's **centro storico** (old historic center). This was the core of medieval Rome, and is where the heart of modern Rome still beats strongly. Here you will find some of the best restaurants, boutiques, and sights, sounds and smells that will make your visit to Rome memorable. Take the time to wander these streets and you will have sampled something special. Refer to the three walking tours later in the book dedicated to helping you explore this area.

11. Colonna di Marcus Aurelius
Piazza Colonna. Metro-Barberini.

Carved between 180 and 196 CE, this column is a continuous spiral of bas-reliefs celebrating Marcus Aurelius' military victories. Statues of Marcus Aurelius and his wife once adorned the top of the column, but in the 16th century they were replaced by the statue of Saint Paul. Today this piazza has been made into another of Rome's car-free zones, since the citizens of this city, as well as other cities in Europe, are realizing that life is a lot more peaceful without cars zooming everywhere.

12. Campo dei Fiori
Web: www.roma2000.it/zcampo.html. Buses 46, 62, 64, 65, 70.

This is a typically Roman piazza that hosts a lively flower and food market every morning until 1pm, except Sundays. Here you'll hear the cries of the vendors blending with the bargaining of the customers. Though there are now some booths specifically catering to tourists, the majority of the stands are for the

SIGHTS 19

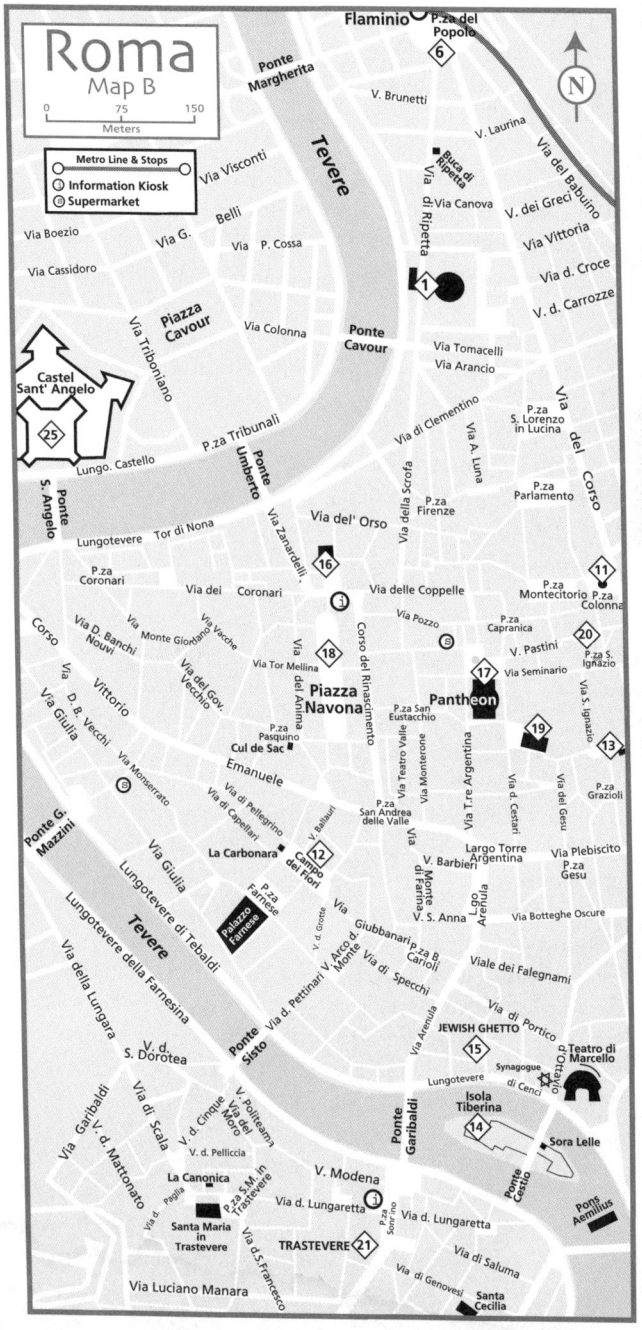

locals, as are the majority of the shoppers. A perfect place to catch a glimpse of authentic Roman life.

The campo used to serve as the spot where heretics were burned at the stake and criminals were hanged. The monument in the middle is in memory of Giordano Bruno, a famous philosopher who was immolated here in 1600.

13. Galleria Doria-Pamphili
Piazza del Collegio Romano 1a, Tel. 06/679-7323; Web: www.doriapamphilj.it. Open 10am-5pm, closed Thursday, €8 museum, €4 private apartments (these are only open 10:30am to noon).

This private collection just off the Via del Corso was recently reopened to the general public. Here you can tour an incredible private art museum and a number of period apartments dolled up with exquisite furnishings. Works by Caravaggio, Titian, Velasquez and other masters are included. Some say Velasquez's Portrait of Innocent X, done in 1650, is the single greatest painting in Rome. The audio tour in English is recommended.

14. Isola Tiberina
Web: www.roma2000.it/ztiberin.html. Buses 44, 75, 170, 710, 718, 719.

Located on the way to Trastevere, this island used to be a dumping ground for dead and sick slaves. Also, at that time, in the 3rd century BCE, there was a sanctuary here to the Greek God of healing, Askleapios.

Currently half the island is taken up by the hospital of Fatebene Fratelli showing that traditions do live on. The church on the island, San Bartolomeo was built in the 12th century, and was substantially altered in the seventeenth. The whole island is a great place to relax with wide walkways along the river. The remains of the Pons Aemilius, the oldest bridge in Rome washed away by a flash floor in 1598, can be seen south of the island. The oldest surviving bridge in Rome is the Ponte Fabricio leading from the island to the Jewish Ghetto. It was built in 62 BCE

15. Jewish Ghetto
Buses 780, 774, 717.

The ancient Jewish quarter is a peaceful riverside neighborhood with narrow curving streets and ocher apartment buildings. It looks much like any other section of Rome until closer inspection reveals Kosher food signs and men wandering around with skull caps. Technically the Ghetto ceased to exist in 1846 when its walls were torn down, but the neighborhood remains home to Europe's oldest and proudest Jewish community.

The history of the Jews in Rome dates back to 161 BCE when Judas Maccabaeus sent ambassadors to Rome to seek protection against the Syrians. Over time many traders followed these emissaries and a Jewish community sprouted.

After Rome colonized and eventually conquered the Land of Israel culminating in 70 CE with the fall of Jerusalem and the destruction of its Temple (an event etched in stone on the Arch of Titus), as many as 40,000 Jews settled in Rome. They contributed to all aspects of Roman society and they and their religion were accepted as different but equal until Christianity became the religion of the state. At which point discrimination against the Jews became widespread.

In the 13th century, for instance, the Catholic Church ordered Jews to wear a distinctive sign on their clothing: a yellow circle for men and two blue stripes for women. Anti-Semitism continued to grow to the point where in 1556, Pope Paul IV confined all Jews to this small section of the city and closed it in with high walls. This was not the first imprisonment of its kind. The Venetians did the same thing to its Jewish population four decades earlier. In Venice the Jews were forced to live on the site of an old cannon foundry, or *getto*. The name stuck and has since evolved to mean any section of a city that is composed of one type of activity, or is inhabited by one group of people.

Today there are over 16,000 Jews living in Rome and the Ghetto is still their central meeting place. To find out more about this neighborhood stop in the Jewish Museum in the **Sinagoga** *(Lungotevere de Cenci, Tel. 06/684-0061, Fax 06/6840-0684; open 9:00am-6:30pm Tuesday-Friday, until 8:00pm on Sundays and also from 9:00pm-midnight on Saturdays in the summer. English tours €7.).* Inside you will find a plan of the original ghetto, as well as artifacts from the 17th century Jewish community.

16. Palazzo Altemps
Piazza Sant'Appolinare 44, Tel. 06/683-3759. Web: www.comune.roma.it/monumentiantichi/monumenti/altemps.htm. Open 9:00am-9:00pm Tues-Thurs and until midnight every other day except Monday when it is closed. Admission €5. Buses 70, 81, 87, 90.

Located just outside the Piazza Navona, this small museum has an elegant collection of ancient Roman and Greek sculptures. Besides the excellent pieces inside, the building itself offers a glimpse into what life was like many years ago in Rome. The inner courtyard is mesmerizing and the private chapel an oasis of calm. Though it does not have as many pieces as the Vatican or the Campidoglio, you will able to savor each work here without having to fight the crowds that flock to other museums. A hidden treasure.

17. Pantheon
Piazza della Rotonda. Tel. 06/6830-0230. Web: www.roma2000.it/zpanthe.html. Open Monday-Saturday 9:00am-6:30pm, Sundays 9:00am-1:00pm. At 10:00am on Sundays is a mass. Tel. 06/6830-0230. Buses 70, 81, 87, 90.

Located in a vibrant piazza, the Pantheon is one of the most famous and best-preserved monuments of ancient Rome. Besides the architectural beauty, the entrance area to the Pantheon is by far the coolest place in Rome during the heat wave of August. So if you want to relax in icy comfort in the middle of a hot day, park yourself under the portico.

First constructed by Agrippa in 27 BCE, the Pantheon was restored after a fire in 80 CE and returned to its original rotunda shape by the Emperor Hadrian. In 609 CE, it was dedicated as a Christian Church and called Santa Maria Rotunda. In the Middle Ages it served as a fortress. In 1620 the building's bronze ceiling was removed and melted into the cannons for Castel Sant'Angelo and used for Bernini's Baldacchino (Grand Canopy) in Saint Peter's. The building is made up of red and gray Egyptian granite, and each of the sixteen columns is 12.5 meters high and is composed of a single block of stone.

You enter the building by way of the original bronze doors. As you enter, it is impossible not to feel the perfect symmetry of space and harmony of the architectural lines. The marvelous dome (diameter 43 meters) is inspiring, even with the hole in the middle that allows rain in during moments of inclement weather.

There are three niches in the building that contain tombs: Victor Emmanuel II (died 1878), one of Italy's few war heroes, Umberto I (died 1900) and Queen Margherita (died 1926), and in another niche the tomb of renowned artist whose last name of Sanzio is not nearly as well known as his first, Raphael (died 1520).

18. Piazza Navona
Web: www.roma2000.it/znavona.html. Buses 70, 81, 87, 90.

This piazza is on the site of a stadium built by Domitian in 86 CE that was used for mock naval battles, gladiatorial contests, and horse races. The stadium's old north entrance has been excavated allowing us to see some original stone arches located some 20 feet below the current street level. After the Roman era the piazza was lined with small squatters' homes that followed the tiers of the stadium. However, because of its wide open space it soon became a prime spot for upscale buildings. Today the style of the piazza is richly Baroque, featuring works by two great masters, Bernini and Borromini.

Located in the middle of the square is Bernini's fantastic Fontana Dei Quattro Fiumi (Fountain of Four Rivers), sculpted from 1647-51. The four figures supporting the large obelisk (a Bernini trademark) represent the four major rivers known at the time: the Danube, the Ganges, the Nile, and the Plata Rivers.

Within this statue Bernini has hidden a window back in time. Notice the figure representing the Nile shielding its eyes from the facade of the church it is facing, Santa Agnese in Agone. This church was designed by Bernini's rival at the time, Borromini; and Bernini is playfully showed his disdain for his rival's design through the sculpted disgust in his statue.

At the south end of the piazza is the Statue of Il Moro (actually a replica) created by Bernini from 1652-54. To the north is a basin with a 19th century Statue of Neptune struggling with a sea monster. To savor the artistic and architectural beauty, as well as the vibrant nightlife of the piazza, choose a table at one of the local restaurant or cafés and sample some excellent Roman gelato (ice cream), grab a coffee, or have a meal and watch the people go by.

Navona has been one of Rome's many gathering spots for people of all ages since the early 18th century. You'll find local art vendors, caricaturists, hippies selling string bracelets, and much more. The piazza is also home to a fun Christmas fair that lasts from mid-December to mid-January. Filled with booths and performers, it is much like an old fashioned carnival for kids of all ages. This is a piazza you should not miss if you come to Rome.

19. Santa Maria Sopra Minerva
Piazza della Minerva, Tel. 06/ 6990339. Hours 7:00am-7:00pm. Buses 70, 81, 87, 90.

Built on the pagan ruins of a temple to Minerva, this must-see church was begun in 1280 by the Dominican Order that also commissioned the beautiful Santa Maria Novella in Florence. With their wide Gothic vaulted nave and aisles, the two churches are very similar in design.

In this expansive church, you can find many tombs of famous personages of the 15th through the 16th centuries as well as beautiful paintings, sculptures, frescoes and bas-relief work. The main attraction are the remains of Saint Catherine of Siena, who died in Rome in 1380, that now reside at the high altar.

To the left of the altar is the statue of Christ Carrying the Cross created by Michelangelo in 1521. The bronze drapes were added later for modesty. If you compare this work to the one to the right of the altar, John the Baptist by Obici, you can easily see why Michelangelo is considered a master. His statue looks as if it could come to life, while the one by Obici simply appears carved out of stone.

Behind the altar are the tombs of Pope Clement VII and Leo X, created by the Florentine sculptor Baccio Bandanelli. In the Sacristy is a chapel covered with frescoes by Antoniazzo Romano, brought here in 1637 from the house where Catherine of Siena died.

In front of the church is a wonderful sculpture of an elephant with an obelisk on his back called Il Pulcino, which was designed by Bernini and carved by Ercole Ferrata.

20. Tempio di Adriano
Piazza di Pietra. Buses 56, 60, 62, 85.

Located near Piazza Colonna and the Via del Corso, the Temple of Hadrian is a fantastic example of architectural pastiche where structures from different eras are blended together into one building. In this case, one wall of the modern Roman Stock Exchange (Borsa) has eleven Corinthian columns from the temple dedicated by Antonius Pius to his father Hadrian in 145 CE.

Note the path that runs in front of this sight. It leads to the Trevi Fountain and the Pantheon, and is marked with signs. By building this pathway and erecting these signs, Romans have finally decided to acknowledge that their entire city is a museum.

21. Trastevere
Tram 8 from Largo Argentina.

This is the perfect place to immerse yourself in Roman life. Trastevere literally means "across the river" and here you'll find interesting shops and boutiques, and plenty of excellent restaurants among the small narrow streets and piazzette (small squares). Trastevere is a great place to enjoy the ease of Roman life. During the month of July the Trasteverini express their feeling of separation from the rest of Rome with their summertime festival called Noiantri, meaning "we the others," in which they mix wine-induced revelry with religious celebration in a party of true bacchanalian proportions.

Santa Maria in Trastevere
Piazza Santa Maria in Trastevere 1, Tel. 06/581-4802. Web: www.roma2000.it/ztraste.html. Hours 7:00am-7:00pm. Tram 8 from Largo Argentina.

This was one of Rome's earliest churches and the first to be dedicated to the Virgin Mary. It was built in the 4th century and remodeled between 1130-1143. The Romanesque belltower was built in the 12th century. Best known for its prized mosaics, especially the 12th and 13th century representation of the Madonna that adorns the facade of the church. The interior is of three naves separated by columns purloined from ancient Roman temples.

On the vault you'll find exquisite mosaics depicting the Cross, emblems of the Evangelists, and Christ and the Madonna enthroned among the Saints (created by Domenichino in 1140). Lower down, the mosaics of Pietro Cavallini done in 1291 portray in six panels the life of the Virgin.

Santa Cecilia in Trastevere
Via Anicia. Open Tue and Thu 10am-noon and 4-5.30pm. Tram 8 from Largo Argentina. Crypt €2.

Santa Cecilia's was founded in the fifth century and had a make over in the ninth century as well as the 16th. A baroque doors leads to a picturesque court, beyond which is a baroque facade, with a mosaic frieze above the portico, and a beautiful bell tower erected in the 12th century. There are several important works of art to be found in the church, not the least of which is the expressive statue of Santa Cecilia by Stefano Maderno. It represents the body of the saint in the exact position it was found when the tomb was opened in 1559.

Another place of interest to visit on the church grounds is the Roman house where Santa Cecilia suffered her martyrdom. There are two rooms preserved, one of them has the bath where she died. It still has the pipes and large bronze cauldron for heating water; which is how she was martyred, with boiling water and steam, lobster-style. A great church to visit, not just for the art, but also for the history.

The Vatican

Vatican City, which consists of St. Peters and Vatican Museums, was once the center of a worldly empire that extended south halfway to Naples and north along the Adriatic past Ravenna. Known as the Papal States, it was only the creation of the modern country of Italy in 1870 that shrunk the power of the papacy down into this

SIGHTS 27

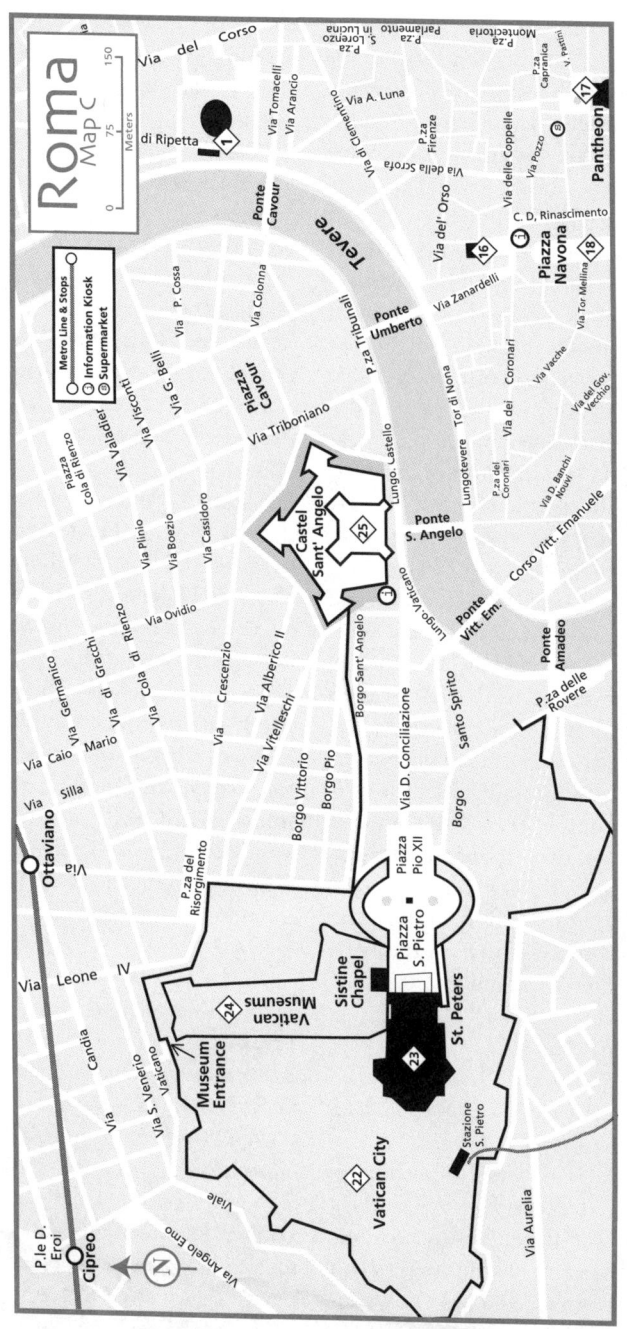

tiny little principality. The Vatican is one of two sovereign states contained within the borders of Italy. The other is San Marino near Bologna.

Today the Vatican is the seat of the Roman Catholic Church, and within these fortress walls are riches beyond all imaginings. The wealth created by centuries of artistic patronage fills the Vatican Museums, and priceless books and documents that chronicle the rise and fall of empires are stashed away in climate controlled storerooms. Then there are the valuable jewels, gold bullion, and real estate deeds for the church properties all over the world stashed deep inside the Vatican bank vaults. Estimates put the value of the Vatican City and all it contains at over 48 billion dollars. Even if you are not Catholic or even remotely religious, a trip to Rome is not complete with a visit to the Vatican, its museums, and St. Peter's.

22. Vatican City
Piazza San Pietro. Metro-Ottaviano. Web: www.vatican.va.

The Vatican (officially referred to as The Holy See) is a completely autonomous country within the Italian Republic and has its own radio and television stations, railway, newspaper, stamps, money, and diplomatic representatives in major capitals. Though it doesn't have an army, the Swiss Guards have been protecting the pope for centuries. Today we think of the Swiss as pacifists, having remained neutral during WW II. But centuries ago the Swiss were Europe's fiercest warriors. The Swiss Guards are a reminder of that.

La Citta Vaticano sits on the right bank of the Tiber river, in the foothills of the Monte Mario and Gianicolo section of Rome. In ancient Rome this was the site of the Gardens of Nero and the main circus where thousands of Christians were martyred. Saint Peter met his fate here around 67 CE. Today it is the world center for the Catholic Church, rich in priceless art, antiques, and spiritual guidance.

23. San Pietro–Saint Peter's
Piazza San Pietro. Hours 8:00am-6:00pm, but only until 5:00pm in the winter. Tel. 06/6988-4466. Metro-Ottaviano.

Located in the monumental square Piazza San Pietro, Saint Peter's is a masterpiece created by Bernini between 1655 and 1667, and is the largest church in the world. The piazza in front is an ovoid shape 240 meters at its largest diameter. It is composed of 284 massive marble columns, and 88 pilasters forming three galleries 15 meters wide. Surrounding the piazza, above the oval structure are 140 statues of saints.

If you stand on the two porphyrys (disks) in the ground in St. Peter's Square, located on either side of the obelisk, and look at the columns (which run four deep) surrounding the square, the architectural brilliance of this piazza is displayed. Only one column is visible from each row of four.

In the center is an obelisk 25.5 meters high with four bronze lions at its base, all of which were brought from Heliopolis during the reign of Caligula (circa 40 CE) and which originally stood in the circus of Nero. Below the monument you can see the points of the compass and the names of the winds.

The church of Saint Peter's rises on the site where Peter the saint is buried. The early Christians erected a small oratory on the site of the tomb, but that was destroyed in 326 when Constantine the Great erected the first Basilica on this site. Over the centuries the church began to expand and became incongruously and lavishly decorated, so that by 1452 Pope Nicholas V decided to make it more uniform. He commissioned Bernardo Rossellino to design a new structure. When that Pope died three years later this work was interrupted, but in 1506 Pope Julius II, with the assistance of Bramante, continued the work on a grander scale.

Then Bramante died in 1514 before his work could be finished. His successor was Raphael, and when he died four years later, Baldassare Peruzzi and Antonio de Sangallo the Younger took over the responsibility jointly. Work was interrupted by the sack of Rome in 1527, then again in 1536 when Peruzzi died. When Sangallo died in 1546, the project was taken over and modified by the 72-year old Michelangelo. Before he died eight years later, Michelangelo had modified Bramante's plan for the dome and we are blessed with his pointed Florentine version today. It would appear that his design is modeled after Brunelleschi's brilliant dome on the Duomo in Florence. After Michelangelo brilliant life was over, the plans he made for St. Peter's were more or less adhered to by his successors who designed the facade according to his plan. On November 1, 1626, Urbano VIII dedicated the Basilica as we know it today.

Note: One of the best ways to see St. Peter's is on a free English-language tour of the basilica by trained volunteer guides. Available seven days a week, Monday-Saturday at 3:00pm and Sundays at 2:30pm, the tour lasts an hour and a half and offers an indepth historical and religious perspective of this magnificent church. The tours start at the information desk to the right as you enter the portico of St. Peter's. *For more information, call 06/6972.*

The Facade

Rounding off, the facade is 115 meters long and 45 meters high, and is approached by a gradually sloping grand staircase. At the sides of this staircase are the statues of Saint Peter (by De Fabis) and Saint Paul (by Adamo Tadolini). On the balustrade, held up by eight Corinthian columns and four pilasters, are the colossal statues of the Savior and St. John the Baptist surrounded by the Apostles, excluding Saint Peter. There are nine balconies, and from the central one the Pope gives his Christmas and Easter benedictions.

The Interior

The church is more than 15,000 square meters in area, 211 meters long and 46 meters high. There are 44 altars and 229 marble columns: 133 of travertine, 16 of bronze, and 90 of stucco.. On the floor of

---

JAZZ IT UP IN ROME

Alexander Platz
Via Ostia 9, Tel. 06/3974-2171. Membership entry €6. Nearest Metro: Ottaviani.

Located near St. Peter's this is without a doubt the best jazz club in Rome. For 16 years it has hosted top quality acts, gaining for itself national and international renown. The walls are covered with photos of the musicians who have played here. Dinner is served. Concerts every evening starting at 10:30pm.

SIGHTS 31

the central nave you'll find lines drawn identifying where other churches in the world would fit if placed in Saint Peter's. Also on the floor, near the front entrance, is a red disk indicating the spot where Charlemagne was crowned Holy Roman Emperor by Leo III on Christmas Day in 800 CE. To the right of this, in the first chapel, is the world famous Pieta created by Michelangelo in the year 1498 when he was only 24.

In the niches of the pilasters that support the arches are statues of the founders of many religious orders. In the last one on the right you'll find the seated bronze statue of Saint Peter. The statue's foot has been rubbed by so many people for good luck that its toes has all but disappeared.

Just past the statue is the grand cupola created by Michelangelo. One of the most amazing architectural wonders of all times, it is held up by four colossal spires which lead to a number of open chapels. Under the cupola, above the high altar rises the famous Baldacchino (or Grand Canopy) made by Bernini, and constructed of bronze taken mainly from the roof of the Pantheon. In front of the altar is the Chapel of Confessions made by Maderno, around which are 95 perpetually lit lamps illuminating the Tomb of Saint Peters. In front of the shrine is the kneeling Statue of Pius VI made by Canova in 1822.

Throughout the rest of the Basilica you'll find a variety of superb statues and monuments, many tombs of Popes, and a wealth of chapels, not the least of which is the Gregorian Chapel designed by Michelangelo and executed by Giacomo della Porta. It is rich in marbles, stuccos, and mosaics, all put together in the creative Venetian style by Madonna del Soccorso in the 12th century.

One controversial tomb is that of Pope Celestine V who allegedly died at the hands of his overeager successor, Boniface VIII. Researchers were recently granted permission to x-ray the tomb and it clearly showed that a ten-inch nail was driven into the Celestine's skull.

If you grow tired of the many beautiful works of art and wish to get a bird's eye view of everything, you can ascend into Michelangelo's Cupola either by stairs (537 of them) or by elevator. The views from the top over the city of Rome are magnificent.

The Vatican Underground
If you are looking for a unique adventure below St. Peter's Basilica that not many people know about, try the Scavi (underground) tour. You'll find mysterious bones, uncovered graves, ancient foundations, and tons of archeological intrigue. But you need to reserve well in advance, and the reservation process is just as secretive as the Scavi Tour is unknown. For specific information about reservations access www.vatican.va, click on the "The Holy See," then the unlabelled "Roman Curia" icon (it's the top circular icon). Next select "Institutions Connected With the Holy See," followed by "Excavations Office." *Admission is €10 and well worth the price. If you do not have internet access, the fax number is 011-39-06-6987-3017, or the address is Fabbrica of St. Peter, 00120 Vatican City.*

24. Vatican Museums
Viale Vaticano, Tel. 06/6988-4466. Admission €12. Web: www.vatican.va. From November-March and June-August open 8:45am to 12:20pm. From March-June and September-October open 8:45am to 3:20pm. Closed most Sundays and all major religious holidays such as Christmas and Easter. The last Sunday of every month in January, February, April, May, July, Aug., September, October, November and December the entrance is free. Metro-Ottaviano.

The Vatican Museums keep rather short hours, and does not make reservations ahead of time for visiting the Museums and/or Sistine Chapel. Those who would like to avoid walking long distances or standing on long lines, choose a tour company and make a

---

CAFE WITH A VIEW

Jesus may have thrown the money changers out of temple, but recently the Vatican opened a cafe on the top of Chistendom's largest church that offers light snacks and drinks, as well breathtaking views over St. Peter's Square, the Tiber River and beyond. Accessible on the way down from the dome, the atmosphere is well, heavenly. This is a great place to take a break.

reservation to join a private, group tour in English. There are also a number of self-guided tape cassette tours available that take you through different sections of the Vatican Museums.

Pinacoteca Vaticana

A wonderful collection of masterpieces from many periods, covering many styles all the way from primitive to modern paintings. Here you can find paintings by Giotto, many works by Raphael, the famous Brussels Tapestries with episodes from the Acts of the Apostles created by Pieter van Aelsten in 1516 from sketches by Raphael, and countless other paintings with religious themes.

Pius Clementine Museum

Founded by Pius VI and Clement XIV and known mainly as a sculpture museum, you can also find mosaic work and sarcophagi from the 2nd, 3rd and 4th centuries. One mosaic in particular is worth noting, the Battle between the Greeks and the Centaurs, created in the first century CE. Also worth noting is the bronze statue of Hercules and the Hall of the Muses that contain statues of the Muses and the patrons of the arts. Here you can also find many busts of illustrious Romans including Caracalla, Trajan, Octavian and more.

In the Octagonal Court is the Cabinet of the Laocoon, which portrays the revenge of the gods on a Trojan priest, Laocoon, who had invoked the wrath of the gods by warning his countrymen not to admit the Trojan horse. In revenge the gods sent two enormous serpents out of the sea to destroy Laocoon and his two sons.

Chiaramonti Museum

Founded by Pope Pius VII, whose family name was Chiaramonti, this museum includes a collection of over 5,000 Pagan and Christian works. Here you can find Roman Sarcophagi, Silenus Nursing the Infant Bacchus, busts of Caesar, the Statue of Demosthenes, the famous Statue of the Nile with the 16 boys representing the 16 cubits of the annual rise of the Nile, as well as a magnificent Roman chariot recreated in marble by the sculptor Franzone in 1788.

Etruscan Museum

If you can't make it to any of the Necropoli around Rome, at least come here and see the relics of a civilization that preceded Ancient Rome. Founded in 1837 by Gregory XVI, this museum contains objects excavated in the Southern part of Etruria from 1828-1836, as well as pieces from later excavations around Rome. Here you'll find an Etruscan tomb from Cervetri, as well as bronzes, gold objects, glasswork, candelabra, necklaces, rings, funeral urns, amphora and much more.

Egyptian Museum

Created by Gregory XVI in 1839, this museum contains a valuable documentary of the art and civilization of ancient Egypt. There are sarcophagi, reproductions of portraits of famous Egyptian personalities, works by Roman artists who were inspired by Egyptian art, a collection of wooden mummy cases and funeral steles, mummies of animals, a collection of papyri with hieroglyphics, and much more.

Library of the Vatican

Founded through the efforts and collections of many Popes, this museum contains many precious documents. Today the library contains over 500,000 volumes, 60,000 ancient manuscripts, and 7,000 incunabuli, including the valuable Codex Vaticanus B, a 4th century Bible in Greek.

Appartamento Borgia

Funded by Pope Alexander VI, whose family name was Borgia, from the furnishings to the paintings to the frescoes of Isis and Osiris on the ceiling, this little "museum" is worth a look.

Sistine Chapel

The private chapel of the popes, famous for ceiling painted by Michelangelo. Started in 1508 and finished four years later, on the ceiling you'll find scenes from the Bible, among them the Creation, where God comes near Adam, who is lying down, and with a simple touch of his hand imparts the magic spark of life. You can also see the Separation of Light and Darkness, the Creation of the Sun and Moon, Creation of Trees and Plants, Creation of Adam, Creation of Eve, The Fall and the Expulsion from Paradise, the Sacrifice of Noah and his Family and the Deluge.

On the wall behind the altar is the great fresco (20 meters by 10 meters) of the Last Judgment also by Michelangelo and commissioned by Clement VII. Michelangelo was over 60 years of age when he started the project in 1535. He completed it seven years later in 1542.

SIGHTS 35

Worthy of note is that Michelangelo painted people he didn't like in situations with evil connotation in this fresco. The figure of Midas, with asses' ears, is the likeness of the Master of Ceremonies of Paul III, who did not get along well with the artist.

Also worthy of note, is that Pope Pius IV instructed Daniele da Volterra to paint clothing on some of Michelangelo's most prominent nude figures. These changes were left in when the entire chapel underwent its restoration a few years back that brought out the vibrant colors of the original frescoes that had been covered by centuries of dirt and soot.

Rooms of Raphael

Initially these rooms were decorated with the works of many artists of the 15th century, but because Pope Julius II loved the work of Raphael so much, he had the other paintings destroyed, and commissioned Raphael to paint the entire room himself. He did so, spending the rest of his short life in the task. Not nearly as stupendous as the Sistine Chapel work by Michelangelo, but it still is one of the world's masterpieces.

Chapel of Nicholas V

Decorated with frescoes from 1448-1451 by Giovanni da Fiesole. The works represent scenes from the life of Saint Stephan in the upper portion and Saint Lawrence in the lower.

The Loggia of Raphael

Divided into 13 arcades with 48 scenes from the Old and New Testaments, these were executed from the designs of Raphael by his students, Giulo Romano, Perin del Vaga, and F. Penni. The most outstanding to see are the Creation of the World, Creation of Eve, The Deluge, Jacob's Dream, Moses Receiving the Tablets of Law, King David, and the Birth of Jesus.

Grotte Vaticano

You need special permission to enter the Vatican caves. If you haven't made plans prior to your arrival it is quite difficult to gain access at short notice. To gain permission you need to contact the North American College in Rome *(Via dell'Umita 30, Tel. 06/ 672-256 or 678-9184, Web: www.pnac.org)*.

The Grotte were dug out of the stratum between the floor of the actual cathedral and the previous Basilica of

Constantine. After passing fragments of inscriptions and mosaic compositions, tombstones, and sarcophagi, you descend a steep staircase to get to the Lower Grottos, also called the Grotte Vecchie (the Old Grottos).

Here you'll find pagan and Christian Necropoli dating from the 2nd and 3rd century. Divided into three naves separated by massive pilasters that support the floor of St. Peter's above, along the walls are numerous tombs of popes and altars adorned with mosaics and sculptures.

25. Castel Sant'Angelo
Lungotevere Castello 50, Tel. 06/3996-7600. Web: w w w . r o m a 2 0 0 0 . i t / zmusange.html. Admission €5. Open 9:00am-7:00pm. Closed Mondays. Metro-Lepanto.

Though not technically part of the Vatican, this castle is still connected to that Holy City by a covered walkway. Because of the volatile political situation in Italy for many centuries, this walkway was used more than once to whisk the Pope to the protection offered by Castel Sant'Angelo. Also known as the Mausoleum of Hadrian since it was built as a tomb for Hadrian and his successors, it was used for eighty years as a funeral monument where the ashes of Roman emperors were stored. As the papacy began to establish itself near the tomb of St. Peter's during the Middle Ages, the structure was converted into a fortress for the Popes. During that period the bulky battlements and other military fortifications were added. Since then it has been used as a residence for popes and princes, as a prison, and as a military barracks.

On the summit of the building is the statue of an angel (hence the name of the castle), and rumor has it that in 590 CE, Gregory the Great saw a vision with an avenging angel sheathing its sword at the summit of the castle. He took this to mean the plague that had ravaged Rome was over. To commemorate this event he placed an angel on top of the building. Today the castle houses a museum with a wonderful collection of armaments from the Stone Age to the present day. There are also some nondescript art exhibits and luxuriously preserved Papal apartments. A great site for kids and adults to explore.

Around the Forum

Life in the ancient Roman Empire revolved around the Forum. Business was conducted, policies made, slaves traded, vestal virgins ogled, gossip shared, all within the shadow of the columns, buildings, temples and marketplaces of the Forum. To come here today is to quite literally walk back in time. Though much of what remains is in ruins, the structures still evoke an inspiring grandeur. Any trip to modern Rome is incomplete without a journey through the remnants of ancient Rome.

26. Arch of Constantine
Piazza Colosseo. Web: www.roma2000.it/zcosta.html. Metro-Colosseo.

Located near the Colosseum, this monument was built in 312 CE to commemorate the Emperor's victory over Maxentius at the Ponte Milvio. Comprised of three archways, this is the largest and best-preserved triumphal arch in Rome.

Even though this is the Arch of Constantine, the attic panels are from a monument to Marcus Aurelius. On one side of the attic the bas-reliefs represent Marcus Aurelius in his battle with the Dacians, and on the opposite side there are scenes commemorating deeds by Marcus Aurelius and Constantine. On the lower areas there are bas-reliefs from earlier arches of Trajan and Hadrian.

27. Baths of Caracalla
Via Terme di Caracalla 52, Tel. 06/3996-7700. Web: www.roma2000.it/zcaracal.html. Admission €5. Hours Monday-Saturday 9:00am until one hour before dark. Mondays and Holidays 9:00am-1:00pm. Metro-Circo Massimo.

Built in 217 CE by the Emperor Caracalla, these baths were second in size only to the Baths of Diocletian. They were used until the sixth century at which time they were destroyed by the invasion of Visigoths. Today it takes quite an imagination to reconstruct the building mentally. The baths were once rich with

38 ROME MADE EASY

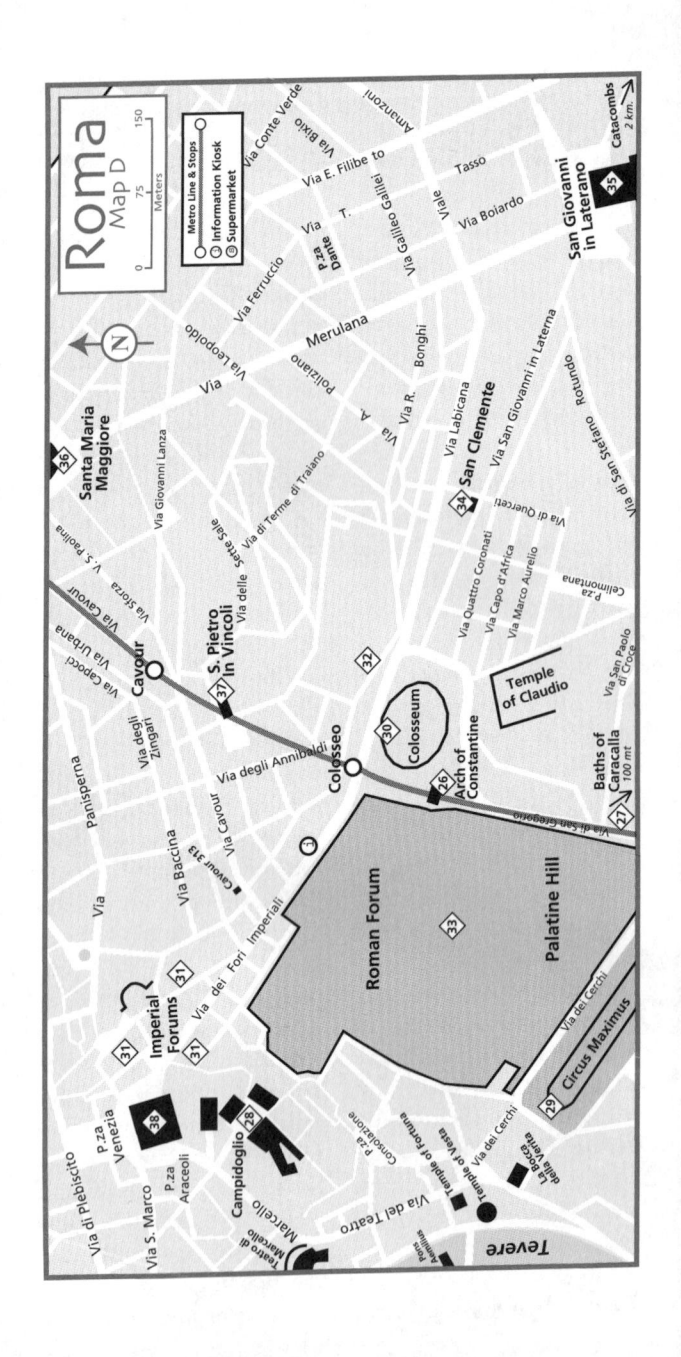

marble and statues and decorated with stucco and mosaic work. All that is left are the weathered remains of the massive brick structure that offers an insight into the scale of the baths, but doesn't offer a glimpse of their beauty. Today, on summer evenings, opera performances are held among the ruins of the Calidarium, the circular vapor bath area.

28. Campidoglio

The Capitoline Hill is one of the seven hills of Rome. It forms the northwest boundary of the Forum and today is home to the Capitoline Museums, which includes the Senatorial Palace and the Palace of the Conservatori. Also located here is the Church of Santa Maria D'Aracoeli (formerly the Temple of Juno Moneta), and the bronze statue of Marcus Aurelius. The Palazzo di Senatori (Senatorial Palace) was finished in the beginning of the 14th century; the statue of Marcus Aurelius was placed here in 1528, and the piazza along with the other two buildings were completed in 1570.

To ascend the hill, take either the steep stairway that leads to the church, the winding ramp of the Via delle Tre Pile, or from between the two of these the monumental stairs, Cordonate, which were designed by Michelangelo. At the entrance to these stairs you'll find two imposing Egyptian lions and at the top you'll find the statues of Castor and Pollux.

The church of Santa Maria D'Aracoeli was originally a pagan temple, then in the 12th century it was given its present form with a colonnade of mismatched ancient columns, stolen from a nearby Roman ruin, and a wide nave. The enormous set of stairs in front are one of the church's main features.

The Capitoline Museums

Piazza del Campidoglio 1. Tel. 06/6710-2071, Web: www.museicapitolini.it. Admission €5. Hours 9:00am-7:00pm. Closed Mondays. Metro-Colosseo.

Founded by Popes Clement XII and Benedict XIV it are the perfect place to come to see what ancient Romans looked like Unlike Greek sculpture, which glorified the subject, Roman sculpture captured every realistic characteristic and flaw. Here there are rooms full of portrait busts dating back to the republic and imperial Rome. Whether they were short, fat, thin, ugly, here they remain, warts and all.

Besides the busts, you'll find a variety of celebrated pieces from antiquity including Dying Gaul, Cupid and Psyche, the Faun, and the nude and voluptuous Capitoline Venice. Then in the Room of the Doves you'll find two wonderful mosaics that were taken from Hadrian's Villa many centuries ago. One mosaic is of the doves drinking from a basin, and the other is of the famous masks of comedy and tragedy.

The Palace of the Conservatori is an amalgamation of three distinct collections: the Museum of the Conservatori, the New Museum, and the Pinocoteca Capitolina. It too was constructed by a design from Michelangelo. Here you will find a large stone head, hand and foot that are fragments from a huge seated statue of Constantine. A great place for a photo.

Look for the famous Boy with a Thorn, a graceful Greek sculpture of a boy pulling a thorn out of his foot; the She-Wolf of the Capitol, an Etruscan work of Romulus and Remus being suckled by the mythical wolf of Rome, the death mask bust of Michelangelo; the marble Medusa head by Bernini; the celebrated painting St. Sebastian by Guido Reni that shows the saint with arrows shot into his body; and the famous Caravaggio work, St. John the Baptist.

29. Circus Maximus
Via del Circo Massimo. Web: www.roma2000.it/zcircom.html. Metro-Circo Massimo.

This circus (or circuit, i.e. racetrack) is located on the flat lands to the south of the Palatine Hill. It was erected in 309 CE by the Emperor Maxentius in honor of his deified son Romulus, whose temple is on the Palatine. Then in Imperial times it was expanded, destroyed, enlarged and finally used as a quarry. Despite the lack of artistic accoutrements its shape is clearly visible underneath the contoured grass and earth, and some of the original seats remain at the turning circle of the southwestern end. The slight hump running through the center marks the location of the spina, around which the chariots, and at times runners, would race. In its prime the Circo Massimo could hold between 150,000-200,000 spectators, more than most modern stadiums.

Outside the west end of the track, at the far end of the museum there, Museo di Roma, is the Church of SM in Cosmedin. Famous for the Bocca della Verita (mouth of truth), an old Roman drain cover that now resides under the church's portico. Reputed to grab hold of the hand of the person who, with hand inserted, tells a lie. According to legend, it was once used by Roman husbands to test the their wives faithfulness.

30. Colosseum
Piazza del Colosseo. Admission €6. Web: www.roma2000.it/zcoloss.html. Hours: summer - 9:00am-7:00pm; winter- 9:00am-5:00pm. Metro-Colosseo.

The Colosseum (Flavian Amphitheater) remains the single most recognized monument surviving from ancient Rome. Its construction began in 72 CE by Vespasian on the site of the Stagnum Neronis, an artificial lake built by Emperor Nero near his house on the adjacent Oppian Hill. Over 500 exotic beasts and many hundreds of gladiators were slain in the arena during the building's opening ceremony in 80 CE, which lasted three months. These types of bloody spectacles continued until 405 CE, when they were abolished.

The structure was severely damaged by an earthquake around that time in the fifth century CE and saw some use afterwards as a theater. Since then it has been used as a fortress and as a quarry for construction material for Vatican buildings.

What we see today is nothing compared to what the building used to look like. In its prime it was covered with marble, and each portico was filled with a marble statue of some important Roman.

The Colosseum used to be fully elliptical and could hold over 50,000 people. Each of the three tiers of seats is supported by a different set of columns: Doric for the base, Ionic for the middle and Corinthian for the top. Inside, the first tier of seats was reserved for the tribunes and other dignitaries such as knights (Which is where the Medieval Age got the term for their chivalric representatives. In fact, if you were not aware of it, the plumed helmets, courteous manner, and colorful banners of Medieval knights were all based on ancient Roman officers, their behavior, garb, and emblems). The second tier in the Colosseum was for citizens, and the third tier for the lower classes and slaves. The Emperor, Senators, Government Officials and Vestal Virgins sat on marble thrones on a raised platform that went around the entire arena.

Inside the arena, below where the floor once was, we can see vestiges of the subterranean passages that were used to transport the wild beasts. Human-powered pulley elevators were employed to get the animals up to the Colosseum floor. At times the arena was flooded to allow for the performance of mock naval battles. Unremarkable architecturally, the Colosseum is instead an engineering marvel from the past which deserves our admiration. A great site for kids and adults to explore.

31. Imperial Forums
Via IV Novembre 94, Tel. 06/679-0048. Web: www.roma2000.it/zfori.html. Open 9:00am-8:00pm every day. In summers on Saturday also open until midnight. Metro-Colosseo.

The Imperial Forums were built in the last days of the Republic, when the Roman Forum became inadequate to accommodate the ever-increasing population, and the emperors needed space to celebrate their own magnificence. These forums were used as meeting places for Romans to exchange views, as lively street markets, or as places where official announcements could be proclaimed to the populace. The first was built by Julius Caesar, and those that followed were created by Augustus, Vespasian, Domitian, Trajan, Nerva, and Hadrian.

After the fall of the Roman Empire, they fell into disrepair; and by the time of the Middle Ages and the Renaissance all that was left are the ruins we see today. Gradually, over the centuries, these monumental ruins became covered with soil. Modern excavation began in 1924 by Mussolini's regime as a way of heralding the glory of Italy and thus Mussolini himself.

Trajan's Forum
Located well below current street level, this is the most grandiose of the Forums of the imperial age and reflects the emperor's eclectic taste in art and architecture. Here you

can see one of the finest monuments in these Imperial Forums, Trajan's Column, built to honor the Victories of Trajan in 113 CE. It is over 30 meters high and is covered with a series of spiral reliefs depicting the military exploits of the Emperor against the Dacians in the 1st century CE. At the summit of this large column is a statue of St. Peter that was placed there by Pope Sixtus V in the 17th century.

Trajan's Market
This is a large and imposing set of buildings attached to Trajan's Forum, where people gathered and goods were sold. In the vast semi-circle is where the merchants displayed their wares.

Forum of Caesar
Located near the Roman Forum, on the other side of the Via dei Fori Imperiali (the road itself was built in 1932 on the site of a far more ancient road to more adequately display the monuments of ancient Rome), this was the earliest of the Imperial Forums. It was begun in 54 BCE to commemorate the Battle of Pharsalus, and finished in 44 BCE. Trajan redesigned many parts of this Forum to meet his needs in 113 CE and to celebrate some of his victories.

For example, Trajan added the Basilica Argentaria (Silver Basilica), which was a meeting place for bankers and money changers. Originally a bronze statue of Julius Caesar stood in the center of this Forum. This statue is now located in the Campidoglio.

Forum of Augustus
Built around the time of Christ's birth, this Forum commemorates the deaths of Brutus and Cassius (the traitors who allied against Caesar) at the Battle of Philippi in 42 BCE. Here you'll find some remains of the Temple of Mars, the god of war, including a high podium and some trabeated (horizontally decorated) columns. To the side of the temple you'll find the remains of two triumphal arches and two porticos.

32. Nero's Golden House
Viale della Domus Aurea. Tel. 06/399-67700. Metro-Colosseo. Hours: 9am to 7:45pm summer; 9am to 5pm winter; closed on Tuesdays. Admission €5.

After 15 years of excavations, the Domus Aurea is once again open to public viewing. Also known as Nero's Golden House, the Domus Aurea was built by Nero after the great fire of 64 CE destroyed his first abode, not to mention a great deal of Rome. Nero appropriated a huge amount of land in much of central Rome and had the finest craftsmen of the day work on this structure. Nero only lived in the palace a few short years, after which most of it was abandoned (as a result of the general dislike for Nero) and much of the grounds given back to the people of Rome. You can view eight rooms today, all underground, and admire the vaulted ceilings, extant pieces of frescoes and stone reliefs, beautiful floor mosaics, and pieces of broken sculpture here and there. It's a magnificent building, and well worth a visit.

To visit the Domus Aurea, you must make a reservation at Centro Servizi per l'Archeologia (Via Amendola 2, Metro-Colosseo, Mon-Sat 9am-1pm and 2-5pm). You can also book a reservation in advance before you leave home through Select Italy (Tel. 847/853-1661 in the U.S.; www.selectitaly.com, cost $19). Or, once you're in Rome, call tel. 06-397-499-07. A recorded message in both Italian and English will guide you through the reservation process. The guided tours, both with a guide or with audio-guides, last about 1 hour from 9am to 7pm. Visitors enter in groups of no more than 25, with gaps of 15 minutes between groups. Even in summer, bring a sweater or jacket, as it can be rather chilly at times.

33. Roman Forum & Palatine Hill

Largo Romolo e Remo 1. Tel. 06/699-0110. Admission €6. Web: www.roma2000.it/zforo.html. Open 9:00am-8:00pm and in the summers on Saturday until midnight. Metro-Colosseo.

The Roman Forum lies between the Palatine and Quirinale hills and was first a burial ground for the early settlers of both hills. Later the area became the center for the religious, commercial and political activities of the early settlers. The surrounding area was greatly expanded in the Imperial era when Roman emperors began building self-contained Fora in their own honor. The entire area has been decimated by war, used as a quarry for other buildings in Rome, and has been haphazardly excavated, but is still

SIGHTS 45

a wonder to behold. And it's a great site for kids to explore. The best way to get an overall view of the Roman Forum is from the back of the Campidoglio. In the Roman Forum you'll find the following sights:

Arch of Septimus Severus
Built in 203 CE to celebrate the tenth anniversary of the Emperor Septimus Severus' reign. This triumphal arch is constructed with two lower archways flanking a larger central arch and is the one of the

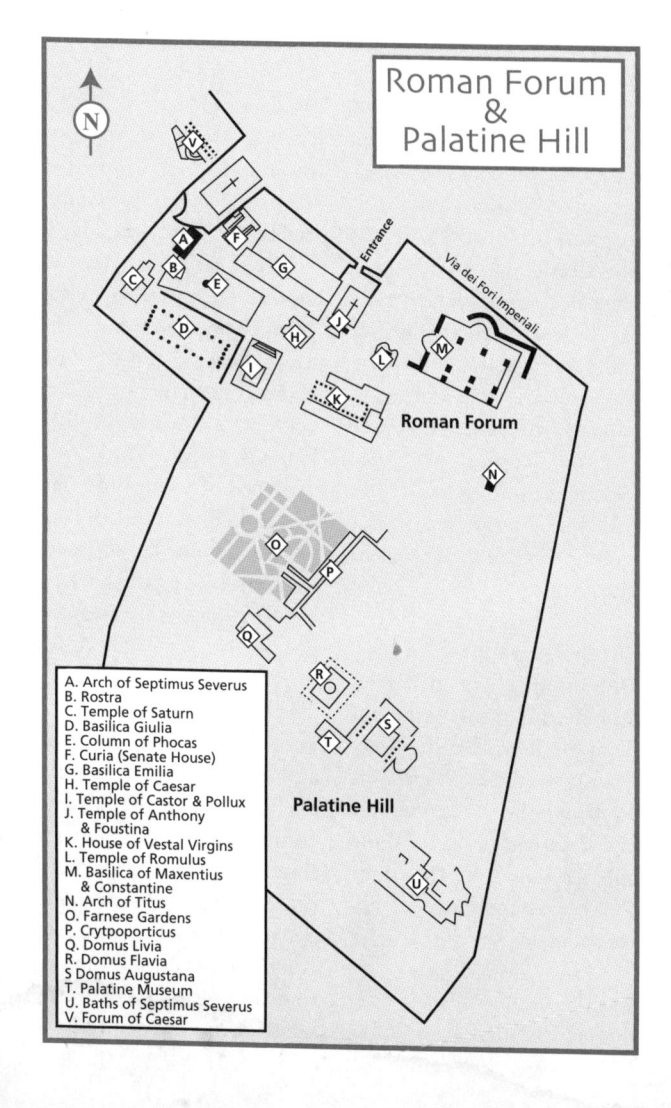

Roman Forum & Palatine Hill

A. Arch of Septimus Severus
B. Rostra
C. Temple of Saturn
D. Basilica Giulia
E. Column of Phocas
F. Curia (Senate House)
G. Basilica Emilia
H. Temple of Caesar
I. Temple of Castor & Pollux
J. Temple of Anthony & Foustina
K. House of Vestal Virgins
L. Temple of Romulus
M. Basilica of Maxentius & Constantine
N. Arch of Titus
O. Farnese Gardens
P. Crytpoporticus
Q. Domus Livia
R. Domus Flavia
S Domus Augustana
T. Palatine Museum
U. Baths of Septimus Severus
V. Forum of Caesar

finest and most imposing structures remaining from ancient Rome. Over the side arches are bas-reliefs depicting scenes from victorious battles fought by the Emperor against the Parthians and the Mesopotamians.

Rostra
Located next to the Arch of Septimus Severus, this building was decorated with the ramrods, or rostra, of ships captured by the Romans at Antium in 338 BCE. It was the meeting place for Roman orators. All that remains now is the semi-circular flight of entry stairs. In front of it is the Column of Phocas, erected in honor of the Eastern Emperor of the Roman Empire, Nicephorus Phocas, in 608 CE. The column was the last monument to be erected in the Forum.

Temple of Saturn
Built in 497 BCE, it was restored with eight ionic columns in the 42 BC that were bounty from the Syrian wars. In the temple's basement was the Treasury of State. Only the threshold of the door which opens towards the Forum remains.

Basilica Giulia
Started in 54 BCE by Julius Caesar on the site of the destroyed Baslica Sempronmia and completed by Augustus, it was destroyed by fire and restored in 12 BCE, then restored a final time in 416 CE. The Basilica consisted of a huge 2 storied hall with five aisles. It once housed the Roman law courts.

Basilica Emilia
Located to the right of the entrance to the Forum, this is the only remaining Republican Basilica and was built in 179 BCE. It was restored on several occasions by Gens Aemilia and now bares his name. Because of the ravages of fire, destruction by barbarian hordes and neglect, little remains today. The facade consisted of a two story portico and 16 arches. It was one of the largest buildings in Rome and was used by money-changers and other business people.

The Curia
Founded by Tullus Hostilius and initially erected between 80 BCE and 44 BCE, it was completed in 29 BCE by Augustus and restored several times. It was the house of the Senate, the government of Rome in the Republican period, and the puppet government during the empire. It

was once covered with exquisite marble but is today a combination of stucco and brick. The structure was rebuilt after a fire in 283 CE, and converted into a church in the seventh century CE. The interior is still a large plain hall, with marble steps that were used as the senator's seats. Take the time to go inside and sit where the Roman Senators sat ages ago. In this room is where many of the major decisions associated with governing Rome were debated.

Temple of Anthony & Faustina

Built by Antonius Pius in honor of his wife Faustina in 141 CE, after his death the temple was dedicated to the emperor as well. The temple was later converted to a church in the 11th century, San Lorenzo in Miranda. All that remains of the original Roman temple are the ten monolithic columns that are 17 meters high, and an elegant frieze. The baroque facade is from the 1600s.

Temple of Caesar

Also known as the Temple of the Divine Julius, this temple was built by Augustus on the site where the body of Julius Caesar was cremated and where Marcus Antonius made his famous funeral oration after the assassination. It was inaugurated on August 18 29 BCE. The little that now remains includes the round altar where the funeral pyre was most likely erected. Septimus Severus restored the Temple after it has been damaged by fire.

Temple of Castor & Pollux

Built in 484 BCE and dedicated to the cult of Castor and Pollux, the temple has been restored many times, most notably by Hadrian and Tiberius. The facade once faced the square of the forum and there were 19 original columns (only three remain). Inside, the Senate would meet periodically to deal with concerns of weights and measures. At the foot of the podium, money changers, bankers and barbers would set up shop.

House of the Vestal Virgins

This is where the vestal virgins lived who dedicated themselves to maintaining the sacred fires in the nearby Temple of Vesta. A portico of two stories adorned with statues of the Vestals surrounded a round open court that was decorated with flower beds and three cisterns. In the court you can still see the remains of some of the statues and the pedestals on which they sat.

Arch of Titus

Erected in 81 CE by Domitian to commemorate the conquering of Jerusalem by Titus. The arch contains bas-reliefs of the Emperor and of soldiers carrying away the spoils of Jerusalem. It is one of the most imposing structures remaining from ancient Rome, and a pilgrimage site for every Jewish tourist to the city.

Temple of Romulus

Once considered as a commemorative building for Romulus, son of Maxentius, who died in 309 CE at a very young age, it is now known as the Temple of Jupiter Stator. The brick construction consists of a domed, round, central location, preceded by a semi-circular face flanked by two rectangular sections. Since the 6th century the temple has been part of the church of Santi Cosma e Damiano.

Basilica of Maxentius

Built between 306 CE and 312 CE by the Emperor Maxentius and completed by Emperor Constantine. The last remaining column was removed in 1613 and placed in front of the Santa Maria Maggiore to commemorate Christianity's dominance over paganism. This is the location where the giant statue of Constantine once stood, the head and foot of which are now on display at the Capitoline Museum.

The Palatine Hill

Of the Seven Hills of Rome, this one's ancient structures have not been paved over with modern progress and new constructs. Once the residence of the Roman emperors during the Golden Age and Imperial Period, it was here, in 754 BCE, that Romulus is said to have founded the city of Rome. However, actual records and not just myth have indicated that settlement was actually established in the 9th century BCE. That's almost 3,000 years ago!

Aristocratic families also resided here, leaving behind wonderful architectural relics most of which have been excavated today, making the Palatine Hill one of the must-see places when you tour the Forum. It is also a wonderful respite from the hectic pace of Rome, filled with lush greenery and plenty of shade.

Entering the Palatine, you pass through the Farnese Gardens. Originally called the Domus Tiberiana, these gardens were laid out in the sixteenth century and were full of orange trees and gurgling fountains. They were created for Cardinal Allessandro Farnese who used them for lavish parties. Underneath the gardens is the Cryptoporticus, a subterranean tunnel built by Nero for hot-weather walks and as a secret route from the Palatine and his palace (Nero's Golden House) across the valley on the Oppian Hill.

Further up the hill is the Domus Livia named after Augustus' wife. The wall paintings here date from the late Republic period. Nearby is the Domus Flavia with the foundations of what appear to be a maze. Next to that is the Domus Augustana, the emperor's private residence. The oval building may have been a garden or a theater for the emperor's private entertainment.

In between the Domus Flavia and Domus Augustana is the Palatine Museum. A nondescript gray building which houses human remains and artifacts from the earliest communities in Rome. In the upstairs rooms are busts and other works from the fourth century CE.

Finally, at the farthest corner of the Palatine lie the remains of the small palace and Baths of Septimus Severus. These are some of the best-preserved buildings on the hill, quite possibly because it was the most difficult point to reach, deterring the scavengers from looting its structure for building materials.

34. San Clemente
Via di San Giovanni Laterano. Admission €2 (to the lower church). Hours to visit the basement 9:00am-1:00pm. Closed Sundays. Metro-San Giovanni.

Located between the Colosseum and St. John Lateran is this hidden gem of a church, San Clemente. One of the better preserved medieval churches in Rome, it was originally built in the fifth century, the Normans destroyed it in 1084 then it was reconstructed in 1108 by Pachal II. Today when you enter you are in what is called the Upper Church, a simple and basic basilica divided by two rows of columns. Above the altar are some intricately inlaid 12th century mosaics.

The Lower Church was discovered in 1857 and contains subterranean passages that housed an early Christian place of worship, from the days when Christians had to practice their religion below ground for fear of persecution. Even further below that are the remains of a temple dedicated to Mithraic, a religion that practiced in the 4th century CE known for their barbaric blood rites. Brought to Rome from Asia Minor in 67 BCE by soldiers of Rome's Legions, this pagan religion became entrenched in the military because of its bonds of violence, fidelity, loyalty and secrecy. Before the Roman Legions adopted it, Mithraic was the religion of Alexander the Great's army. This is a must see church while in Rome. They also have a bucolic little porticoed garden, with a spritzing fountain in the center.

35. San Giovanni in Laterano
Piazza San Giovanni in Laterano 4, Tel. 06/6988-6452. Web: www.roma2000.it/zschgiov.html. Hours: Baptistery: 6:00am-12:30pm and 4:00-7:00pm; Cloisters 9:00am-5:00pm. Metro-San Giovanni.

Another of the great basilicas of Rome. Most people don't realize that this church, and not St. Peter's, is the cathedral of Rome and the whole Catholic world. Established on land donated by Constantine in 312 CE, that first building has long been replaced by many reconstructions, fires, sackings and earthquakes over the centuries. Today, the simple and monumental facade of the church, created by Allessandro Galiliei in 1735, is topped by fourteen colossal statues of Christ, the Apostles, and saints. It rises on the site of the ancient palace of Plautinus Lateranus, one of the noble families of Rome many eons ago.

To get inside, you must pass through the bronze door that used to be attached to the old Roman Senate house. The interior of the church, laid out in the form of a Latin cross, has five naves filled with historical and artistic objects. In total it is 150 meters long and the central nave, which is flanked by 12 spires from which appear 12 statues of the Apostles from the 18th century, is 87 meters long. The wooden ceiling and the marble flooring are from the 15th century.

The most beautiful artistic aspect of the church is the vast transept, richly decorated with marbles and frescoes portraying the Leggenda Aurea of Constantine. One piece of historical interest is the wooden table, on which it is said that Saint Peter served mass.

36. Santa Maria Maggiore
Piazza di Santa Maria Maggiore. Tel. 06/483-195. Web: www.roma2000.it/zschmar.html. Hours 8:00am-7:00pm. Metro-Termini.

Like St. Paul's Outside the Walls, St. Peter's, and St. John Lateran, this is one of the four patriarchal basilicas of Rome. Its name derives from the fact that it is the largest church (maggiore) in Rome dedicated to the Madonna. The facade, originally built in the 12th century, was redone in the 18th century to include the two canon's houses flanking the church. It is a simple two story facade and as such is nothing magnificent to look at

However, the interior, in all its 86 meters of splendor, is worth a visit mainly because of the 5th-century mosaics, definitely the best in Rome, its frescoes, and multi-colored marble. On the right wall of the Papal Altar is the funeral monument to Sixtus V and on the left wall the monument to Pius V, both created by Fontana with excellent bas-reliefs. Opposite this chapel is the Borghese Chapel, so called since the sepulchral vaults of the wealthy Borghese family lie beneath it. Here you'll view the beautiful bas-relief monumental tombs to Paul V and Clement VIII on its left and right walls. Towards the west end of the church is the Sforza Chapel with its intricately designed vault. Pius VI's eerie crypt is below and in front of the main altar.

37. San Pietro in Vincoli
Piazza di San Pietro in Vincoli, Tel. 06/488-2865. Hours 7:00am-12:30pm and 3:30pm-6:00pm. Metro-Cavour.

Located near the Colosseum, this church was founded in 442 by the Empress Eudoxia as a shrine dedicated to preserving the chains with which Herod bound St. Peter in Jerusalem. These chains are in a crypt under the main altar.

But the reason to come to this church is the tomb of Julius II carved by Michelangelo. On it you will find the unforgettable seated figure of Moses. This statue captures the powerful personification of justice and law of the Old Testament. Moses appears as if he is ready to leap to his feet at any moment and pass judgment. You can almost see the cloth covering his legs or his long beard move with the breeze. Flanking Moses are equally exquisite statues of Leah and Rachel also done by Michelangelo. Everything else was carved by his pupils.

38. Vittorio Emanuele II Monument
Piazza Vittorio Emanuele. Buses 70, 81, 87, 90.

A monument to the first king of Italy who died in 1878. Work started in 1885 but was not finished until 1910. To Romans it is affectionately called "The Wedding Cake," since its shape and white marble make it look eerily like a larger version of one. It contains the tomb of the Italian unknown soldier, and is a great place to get a view over the rooftops of Rome. Not as panoramic a scene as from other spots, but still worth dodging traffic to check out. Be very careful as you cross the street. This is a busy piazza.

Outside the Center of Rome

Once you have seen everything else that central Rome has to offer and you're looking for more, you may want to visit some of the places listed below. The Catacombs are an eerie introduction to the days before Christianity became the Roman Empire's official religion. The Museo della Civilta Romana is a history buff's paradise complete with an awesome room-sized scale model of ancient Rome. The Piramide di Gaius Cestius is sight one would expect to find in Cairo. And if you are a church-hound, San Paolo Fuori le Mura is one of Rome's most significant basilicas.

Catacombs
Saint Callistus (Via Appia Antica 110, Tel. 06/513-6725. Closed Wednesday.); San Sebastian (Via Appia Antica 132, Tel. 06/788-7035. Closed Thursday.); Santa Domitilla (Via di Sette Chiese 282, Tel. 06/511-0342. Closed Tuesday.); Admission for each €5. Hours for each 8:30am-12:00pm and 2:30pm-5:00pm. Buses 118 and 218. Web: www.catacombe.roma.it.

Located next door to one another on and around the Via Appia Antica south of the city, these tombs were originally an ancient Roman necropolis. They were then used by the early Christians as a meeting places, and were finally a haven for them from prosecution. Here you can visit the crypts of the Popes, the crypt of Saint Cecilia, the crypt of Pope Eusebius, as well as frescoes dating back to the 3rd century CE. All three are an eerie reminder of the time before Christianity dominated the Western world, a time when Christians were actually the ones being persecuted instead of doing the persecuting. A great site for kids to explore.

The road to the catacombs is the Appia Antica, the most celebrated of all ancient Roman roads which was begun by Appius Claudius Caecus in 312 BCE. The road has been preserved in its original character as have the original monuments. At first it was the chief line of communication between Rome and Southern Italy, Greece, and the eastern possessions of the Roman Empire.

Museo della Civilta Romana
Piazza G Agnelli 10, Tel. 06/592-6135. Web: www.comune.roma.it/museociviltaromana. Open 9:00am-2:00pm Tues-Sat and Sundays & Holidays. Closed Mondays. Admission €6.5. Metro-EUR Fermi.

This museum contains a perfect replica of Rome during the height of empire in the 4th century BCE. This piece is an exquisitely detailed plastic scale model that helps to bring some sense to the ruins that now litter the center of Rome. Even if you are not a museum person, this exhibit is well worth seeing. Ideal for kids of all ages.

The rest of the museum contains little original material, and is made up of plaster casts of Roman artifacts. The museum is located in the section of Rome called EUR (Esposizione Universale di Roma), built with Mussolini's guidance halfway between Rome and its old port of Ostia, in an attempt to reclaim some of Rome's glory and add to its grandeur. EUR has none of the human feel of the rest of Rome, since it is in essence an urban office park with isolated residential areas.

Piramide di Gaius Cestius
Piazzale Ostiense. Metro-Piramide.

Built in 12 BCE as a tomb for

the Praetor Gaius Cestius, this pyramid is a prime indicator that a cult of Egyptology was one of the largest of the pagan religions. Built of brick and rock and covered with limestone, this is one of the more striking structures left from that time period and as such is a great photo op. Located near one of Rome's best preserved gates, Porta San Paolo.

San Paolo Fuori le Mure
Via Ostiense. Church open 7:00am-6:00pm. Cloisters Open 9:00am-1:00pm and 3:00pm-6:00pm. Web: www.roma2000.it/zschpaol.html. Metro-San Paolo.

Located a short distance beyond the Porta Paolo, St. Paul's Outside the Walls (San Paolo Fuori le Mura) is the fourth of the patriarchal basilicas in Rome. It is second only in size to St. Peter's and sits above the tomb of St. Paul. It was built by Constantine in 314 CE and then enlarged by Valentinian in 386 CE and later by Theodosius. It was finally completed by Honorius, his son.

In 1823, the church was almost completely destroyed by a terrible fire and many of its great works of art were lost. Immediately afterward, renovations began and today it seems as magnificent as ever. With the beautiful garden surrounded by the great rows of columns, the palms growing in the center, the gigantic statue of St. Paul, and the facade with mosaics of four prophets (Isaiah, Jeremaih, Ezekial, and Daniel), just getting inside this church is a visual treat.

The interior is 120 meters long and has four rows of columns and five naves. The columns in the central nave are Corinthian that can be identified by their splendidly ornate capitals. The walls contain Medallion Portraits of the Popes from Saint Peter to Pius XI. On the High Altar sits the ancient Gothic tabernacle of Arnolfo di Cambio (13th century) that was saved from the fire in 1823. Saint Paul rests beneath the altar in the confessional. The mosaic in the apse, with its dominating figure of Christ, was created by artists from the Republic of San Marino in 1220.

To the left of the apse is the Chapel of St. Stephen, with the large statue of the saint created by R. Rainaldi, and the Chapel of the Crucifix created by Carlo Maderno. This chapel contains the crucifix which is said to have spoken to Saint Bridget in 1370.

Also laid to rest here is St. Ignatius de Loyola, who took the formal vows that established the Jesuits as a religious order. To the right of the apse is the Chapel of San Lorenzo and the Chapel of Saint Benedict. One other place of note in the church are the cloisters that contain fragments of ancient inscriptions and sarcophagi from the early Christian era.

Ostia Antica
By car, take the Via del Mare (SS8) for about 25 minutes. By metro and train, take Linea B to the Piramide station, then catch the train to Ostia Antica. It takes about 45 minutes from Stazione Termini and costs only €1. Ferry boats leave from the Ponte Marconi on Fri, Sat and Sun (and Tues, Wed and Thurs by reservation) at 9:15am, arriving at Ostia Antica at 1:30pm, returning at 3:45pm. Tickets cost €10 one-way and €11 return. Web: www.battellidiroma.it

If you are interested in seeing an ancient Roman city being excavated and do not have the time to get to Pompeii or Herculaneum near Naples, Ostia Antica presents a picture of Roman life only a shade less vivid.

Founded in the fourth century BCE, Ostia Antica was once the bustling seaport of Ancient Rome, and the mosaic tile floors found here document the great variety of goods and services once available. Commodities included furs, wood, grain, beans, melons, oil, fish, wine, mirrors, flowers, ivory, gold, and silk. Among the services offered were caulkers, grain measurers, maintenance men, warehousing, shipwrights, bargemen, carpenters, masons, mule drivers, stevedores and divers for sunken cargoes.

There were also a wide variety of housing, including large villas, average sized abodes and vast apartment buildings; along with many public amenities including a theater, baths, and a fire department. Ostia Antica gives an excellent notion of what life in the metropolis was like at the height of the Empire. The plan of the city is scenic, monumental and functional. Its backbone is the major east-west street, the Decumanus Maximus, nearly a mile long, which was once colonnaded, and runs from the Porta Romana straight to the Forum.

You enter the excavations in Ostia at the aforementioned

Porta Romana. The Decumanus Maximus, takes you past the well-preserved old **theater** and the **Piazzale dei Corporazione** (Corporation Square), a tree-lined boulevard once filled with over seventy commercial offices of wine importers, ship owners, oil merchants, or rope makers. All of these shops are worth a visit, but the well-preserved laundry and wine shop contain some of the most exquisite mosaic tiled floors representing their trades. A must see stop around this area is the site museum which has many of the excavated statues.

Farther down the Decumanus Maximus you arrive at the **Capitolium**, a temple dedicated to Jupiter and Minerva, located at the end of the **Forum**. The **insulae** (apartment blocks) are of particular interest since they are often four or five stories high. This is where the average citizens lived. Only the wealthy merchants were able to build themselves separate villas. The insulae were well lighted, had running water, and garbage chutes and toilets on each floor. After the Roman Empire fell, the world would not live with such advancements again until the 20th century.

Two private homes of interest are the **House of the Cupid and Psyche**, which is west of the Capitolium, and the **House of the Dioscuri**, which is at the southwest end of town.

Unlike Pompeii or Herculaneum, Ostia was not covered with ash and lava, but was abandoned starting in the 5th century CE because its two harbors were silting up and were thus no longer of use to Rome. My favorite way to tour this site is to leave the already excavated sections and wander through the areas that have not already been dug up. This helps give you an idea as to the amount of labor involved in actually excavating sections, and usually makes for great places to relax. And who knows maybe you'll turn up and ancient artifact or two.

The site is open daily 9:00am–6:00pm in summer, 9:00am–4:00pm in winter. The museum is open one hour less. Admission €5.

Tivoli Gardens
As the three villas are rather spread out, it is recommended to come here either by car or guided tour. By car, take the Via Tiburtina (SS5). A guided tour can be found with Rome's

SIGHTS 57

official tour guide company (www.guideroma.com/English/tivoli-eng.asp, Via Luigi Gadola 3, Tel. 39/06/230-4101) or any number of others.

Tivoli overlooks Rome from its place on the **Sabine Hills**, and is where the wealthy ancient Romans built their magnificent summer villas. The three main sights here are **Villa Adriana** (Hadrian's Villa), **Villa d'Este**, and Villa Gregoriana.

The Villa Adriana's was begun in 125 CE and completed 10 years later, and was at the time the largest and most impressive villa in the Roman Empire. From his travels Hadrian, an accomplished architect, found ideas that he recreated in this palace.

Another villa is the Villa D'Este's, the main draw of which are its many wonderful fountains. The **Owl Fountain** and **Organ Fountain** are especially beautiful, as is the secluded pathway of the **Terrace of the Hundred Fountains**.

The **Villa Gregoriana** is known for the **Grande Cascata** (the Great Waterfall), which is a result of Gregory XVI diverting the river to avoid flooding. The park around the waterfall has smaller ones flowing through a series of grottoes.

Some other nearby villas that are worth a visit if you have the time include:

Villa Adriana, *Bivio Villa Adriana, 3.5 miles southwest of Tivoli. Open Tuesday-Sunday, 9:30am-1 hour before sunset. Closed Mondays. Small fee required.*

Villa d'Este, *Viale delle Centro Fontane. Open Tuesday-Sunday, 9:30am to 1.5 hours before sunset. May-September also open 9:00pm-11:30pm with the garden floodlit. Closed Mondays. Small fee required. Sundays free.*

Villa Gregoriana, *Largo Sant'Angelo. Open Tuesday–Sunday 9:30am to 1 hour before sunset. Closed Mondays. Small fee required. Sundays free.*

2. WALKS

These walks are designed for people of all ages and each should take around 2 hours to complete. They are not too long or strenuous, but if you feel yourself getting tired, stop at any number of outdoor cafes, sit on a bench in a piazza, or head into one of Rome's many churches and catch a breather on a pew. We will visit sights and museums, but mainly the point of these walks is to get you off of the beaten tourist path and allow you to explore areas of the Eternal City that most visitors rarely see.

To really appreciate Rome, the Italian way of life, and the beauty of European urban living is to be surrounded by old buildings, on cobble-stoned streets, and feel yourself embraced by the community-oriented neighborhoods. These walks will help you find those out of the way places where Rome's most authentic experiences are revealed. Note: featured sights are in **red-bold**.

Il Tridente Walk

Featured Sights: *Piazza di Spagna, Spanish Steps, Via Condotti, Altar and Mausoleum of Augustus, Piazza del Popolo, Via del Corso*

There is no better place to start your exploration of Rome than at the same spot where 17th and 18th century visitors would begin theirs: at the **Piazza di Spagna**. We, however, are going to arrive by a rather more modern conveyance than they did: an electricity-powered Metro system versus horse drawn carriages.

60 ROME MADE EASY

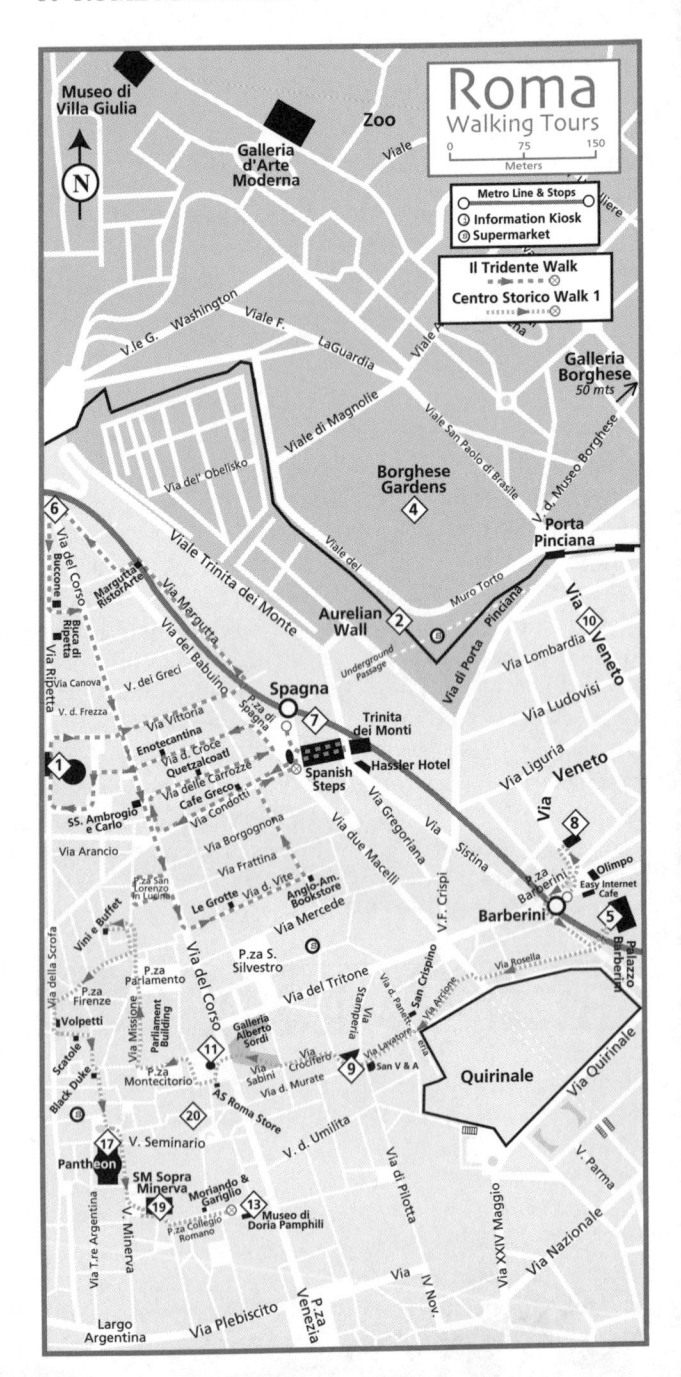

WALKS 61

The Piazza di Spagna gets its name from the Spanish Embassy to the Vatican that was once the most prominent building in this area. The Spanish Embassy is still here, but it has been absorbed by the passage of time and superceded by the temples of commerce that dominate the area now. Before we begin our journey through Rome's haute culture neighborhood, let's first scale the Spanish Steps and get a glimpse of the area we are about to explore.

Since they were built in the 1720s the baroque Spanish Steps have been a main stop on the Grand Tour of Europe, that post-university, pre-adult rite of passage that young aristocrats undertook to expand their horizons prior to settling down to a life of leisure. Cascading from the church of the **Trinita dei Monti**, the Spanish Steps remain a must see stop for modern tourism as well. Especially at Christmas when a crèche is erected half way up the steps, and during spring and fall when the steps are adorned with huge tubs of flowers. At the top of the steps is a world famous luxury hotel:

Hotel Hassler (*Piazza Trinita Dei Monti 6, Web: www.hotelhasslerroma.com*). If you have not had any breakfast, enter the hotel, take the elevator to the top and seek out a table with a breathtaking view over the rooftops of Rome. This is arguably the most wonderful panorama of the city of Rome.

If you've already had breakfast or do not want to venture up to the restaurant, the view from the steps leading up to the church of Trinita dei Monti is a fine substitute.

Built in 1495 with French donations designed to curry favor with the Pope, Trinita dei Monti has two signature bell-towers and an obelisk prominently placed in the front. This single naved church, divided by an iron gate, has the famous fresco by Daniele da Volterra, the Descent from the Cross. Other frescoes inside are by Perin del Vaga and Francesco da Volterra.

At the foot of the steps is a boat-shaped **fountain** designed in 1627 by the famous Gianlorenzo Bernini from which flows delicious aqua that comes here through some still functioning ancient Roman aqueducts. By all means grab a drink from one of the spouts on either end, or fill your water bottle for later.

Directly across the piazza from the steps and past the fountain is the famous shopping street, **Via Condotti**. Here you'll find some high-end stores that need no introduction, including: Gucci (#8), Louis Vitton (#15), Swatch (#33), Giorgio Armani (#76), Cartier (#82), and Prada (#94). In case you missed the memo, this entire area is Rome's luxury shopping district. Right now I can hear the men's groans and feel the women's hearts racing, but this really is a walk made for everyone.

Colloquially known as Il Tridente, the trident, as a result of the shape of the three streets radiating out from the **Piazza del Popolo** (Via di Ripetta, Via del Corso, and Via del Bauino), this area around the Spanish Steps is not just about shopping, it is also about strolling, people watching, admiring the symmetry of place, savoring the peaceful pedestrian zones, and getting a feel for the grand city of Rome.

A visit to this area is not complete without a stop at a great coffee shop:

Caffe Greco (*Via Condotti #86)*. Wonderfully authentic, this cafe is a piece of history, a place where literary luminaries such as Mark Twain, Oscar Wilde, Keats, Shelley, Lord Byron and many more, all sojourned at one time or another.

After the Caffe Greco, on we go down the Via Condotti, through the gauntlet of consumer baubles enticing us to come in and leave a mortgage payment behind for a purchase. Succumb to or ignore the temptation, but soon we will arrive at **Via del Corso**, a main thoroughfare of commerce in Rome.

We will return here later to walk its length, but for now, take a right, walk a bit, and then take another right onto the Via delle Carrozze.

Note: Public restrooms in Rome are few and far between; and in many cases cafes will not allow the public to use their facilities unless something is purchased. This leaves McDonalds as an excellent restroom option while out wandering around. On the left as you enter the Via delle Carrozze is a McDonalds if needed, and with over 60 locations in Rome, there are plenty for those unplanned calls of nature.

> ### RESTAURANT TIP
>
> **Arancio d'Oro**
> *Via Monte d'Oro 17,*
> *Tel. 06/686-5026.*
>
> Near the Via del Corso and the Mausoleum of Augustus is this great local restaurant generally overlooked by tourists. Hidden down a small side street, with a small sign and curtains hindering the view inside people who do not know of it walk right on by. Come here for a true local meal when in Rome.

As you pass by the parked motor scooters, it is somewhat appropriate to know that this street gets its name from the carriage depots it once contained, garaging the vehicles that brought 17th and 18th century travelers to Rome from the north. Along this pleasant street you'll find plenty of store, cafes, and restaurants to satisfy most of your needs, each a unique shopping experience from the next, including a specialty chocolate shop:

Quetzalcoatl *(#26).* Here you can pick some delectable morsels to help fuel your walk or bring home as gifts.

The Via delle Carrozze leads back to the Piazza di Spagna. Once there take a left, then another left onto the Via della Croce.

On this street you'll find more characteristically Roman shops and cafes. If you wish, at any time, take a detour down one of the side streets and explore. And yes, it is safe. Certainly, be smart at night if walking alone, but in general, Rome is safer, by a huge margin than any American city. So explore! Near the end of the Via della Croce on the right is a great wine store:

Enotecantica *(# 76, Web: www.enoteantica.com).* Here you can find any number of vintages to fortify you for the rest of the day.

After our brief snack and libation, let's do some actual sightseeing. You didn't just come to Rome to eat, drink and shop now did you?

Go down the Via della Croce, cross the Via del Corso, go through the Largo dei Lombardi and under an off-white marble *passageway to the **Mausoleum of Augustus.***

This jumble of ruins and overgrown shrubs was once one of the most important monuments in ancient Rome. Originally covered with marble, pillars, and statues, it was originally built to honor Augustus in 28 BCE. Since that time, many other Caesar's joined him in eternal rest inside. During the Middle-Ages the mausoleum became a fortress, then hosted concerts. Finally Mussolini built the fascist style square that surrounds it. Across the piazza on the other side of the mausoleum near the Tiber River is the **Altar of Augustus**, an intricately detailed structure commemorating many aspects of Augustus' life, now on display behind a glass structure. (A building is being constructed around and above the altar to capitalize on Rome's valuable real estate. For the next few years, the altar will be off-limits until construction is completed.)

After this introduction to antiquity, let's go antiquing!

With the altar at our backs and the mausoleum in front, we are going to head around the left side of the mausoleum to the Via Pontefici, cross the Via del Corso, and enter the Via Vittoria.

Via Vittoria contains all sorts of interesting little clothing stores for both men and women. No need to rush, this is still Il Tridente and as such is filled with all manner of sights, sounds, and smells to carry back with you as memories.

At the end of the Via Vittoria we will cross the Via del Babuino, one of the other tines of the Trident and enter the short Via Alibert. Take the first left onto the Via Margutta, Rome's antique and art heaven.

This street is also a tranquil respite from Il Tridente's crowds, and a brief introduction to a high end mixed use, commercial and residential, neighborhood.

*Go all the way to the end, admiring all the antique and art shops. At the Margutta RistorArte(#118), a high end eatery, take a left. At the Via del Babuino turn right. Follow this street to the grandiose **Piazza del Popolo**.*

The obelisk in the center is 24 meters high and came from Egypt during the time of Ramses II in the 8th century

BCE, making it is almost 3,000 years old. It was moved here from the Circus Maximus in 1589.

There are three main churches in this piazza, **Santa Maria del Popolo** abutting the Aurelian Wall at the far end of the piazza from where you are standing. At the start of the trident where you are currently located are two symmetrical baroque churches flanking the intersection of the Via del Corso: **Santa Maria dei Miracoli** (1678), and **Santa Maria in Monesanto** (1675). Both have picturesque cupolas that were begun by C. Rainaldi and finished by Bernini and Carlo Fontana respectively.

Santa Maria del Popolo, though, is the one we're going to visit. It can sometimes look like a half-finished subway station than a cathedral. However it does contain a masterpiece by Caravaggio, "Saints Peter and Paul" (located in the chapel at the end of the left nave); as well as the intriguing **Chigi Chapel** (second chapel on the left) adorned with works by Raphael. Finished entirely in chestnut marble, this chapel in the right light is stunning. It is also a testament to the lasting power of Masonic orders and some say the mysterious cabal called the Illuminati. Filled with the 12 symbols of the Zodiac tied directly to the four elements—Earth, Air, Fire, and Water—and flanked by two pyramids symbolic of pagan worship, these artistic representations are quite odd for a Christian church.

If such earthy, pagan symbolism builds a lusty hunger or thirst in you, there are a number of cafes and restaurants in this piazza from which to choose, including: **Dal Bolognese** *(# 1-2)*, **Canova** *(# 34)*, and **Rosati** *(# 5a)*.

From here lets go down the right hand tine of the trident, Via di Ripetta. Along this street are the following places to consider visiting:

Buccone *(# 19)*. This store may have the best selection of wine in all of Rome. Here you can get a glass of wine or pick up some bottles to bring home.

Buca di Ripetta *(# 36)*. A small, friendly local trattoria that serves excellent Roman cuisine in an authentic atmosphere.

The English Bookshop *(#248)*. Contains an excellent selection of English language books.

*After your meal, glass of wine, or book shopping, take the Via del Vantaggio (note the jumble of a doll hospital shop on the left as you enter the street) back to **Via del Corso** and turn right.*

Time to explore Rome's most popular shopping street. Even though I am not a big shopper, when in Rome it is difficult to ignore the cornucopia of consumer delights. This is especially true on the Via del Corso where the window displays are creative and engaging, most of the shops are unique little boutiques not bland cookie-cutter mall stores, and all offer a wide variety of interesting products.

Just so we don't forget that there is more to Rome than shopping, along the Corso is the church of **Santi Ambrogio e Carlo** *(# 437)*. Built between 1612 and 1685, inside you will find three naves replete with marble and chapels running along either side of the apse. If need be, use the few noteworthy statues and paintings here as an excuse to escape the hectic pace outside.

CAFE TIP

Teichner
Piazza San Lorenzo in Lucina 17,
Tel 06/687-1683.

A classic cafe in a calm and relaxing piazza amid the chaos of Rome. Just off the main shopping street, Via del Corso, situated in one of Rome's most peaceful piazza's, this is a perfect place at which to stop for a break.

---

*After this, keep heading down the Corso until on the right you arrive at my favorite piazza in all of Rome, **Piazza San Lorenzo in Lucina**.*

Not very scenic, but it is a breath of fresh air in the hectic pace of Rome. Make sure to stop in the **Smart Car** dealership *(# 2)* in this piazza. Designed by Swatch and built by Mercedes, these tiny, ever so adorable cars are one of Europe's stylish solutions to high gas prices and automobile congestion. I can't wait for them to come to the U.S.

In this piazza are also some great cafes, including **Vitti** *(# 33)*, **Ciampin** *(#29)*, and my favorite, **Teichner** *(# 17 – see sidebar on previous page).*

After that, head back to the Corso, turn right and when you get to the next street, Via della Vite, turn left. On this street you will find a number of stores and restaurants, including:

Le Grotte *(# 37)*. Known for exquisite pizza's, they also offer a wide variety of delectable dishes, all in a unique cave like setting.

Anglo-American Bookstore *(# 102, Web: www.aab.it)*. A great place to get English language books.

To conclude our little walk through Rome's most famous walking and shopping area, across from the bookstore take the Via M. de' Fiori to the Via Condotti. Take a right and follow this to the Piazza di Spagna where we started the walk..

If you still want to explore the parts we skirted, now's the time to do so. Il Tridente is made for walking and exploring. Come back on your own and snake through these tiny streets where the essence of Rome can be found.

Centro Storico Walk 1

Featured sights: *Piazza Barberini, Palazzo Barberini, Trevi Fountain, Piazza Colonna, Piazza San Lorenzo in Lucina, Pantheon, Santa Maria Sopra Minerva, Galleria Doria Pamphili.*

This walking tour starts in the **Piazza Barberini**. Though this piazza is one of the busiest traffic centers in the city, in the center you will find one of the cities most serene fountains, Fontana del Tritone by Bernini. In this piazza you will also find:

Easy Internet Cafe *(# 2, Web: www.easyinternetcafe.it)*. This is the best place in Rome to get on the internet if you don't have a connection where you are staying.

Olimpo *(# 23, Web: www.berninibristol.com).* This eatery on the top of the five star deluxe Bernini Bristol Hotel has magnificent views over Rome, and is a great place to grab some breakfast, even though it is a tad expensive.

From here go up the Via Veneto on the right hand side (take note of the Lamborghini showroom at #11) to the church of **SM della Concezione** *(#27).* Colloquially know n as the "Church of Bones" in the crypt you will find a macabre display of bones. A truly unique site and a must see destination when in Rome.

*After this go back to the piazza, past the fountain, and take a left up the Via delle Quattro Fontane to the **Palazzo Barberini** (#13, Web: www.galleriaborghese.it/barberini/it.).*

Palazzo Barberini was begun by Carlo Maderno, and eventually was completed by Bernini with the help of a young Borromini. The central structure is by Bernini, but some small windows and the coat of arms are by Borromini. Many of the decoration contain the heraldic symbols of the Barberini: the bees and the sun.

Inside, two stairs lead to the main apartments. The larger one by Bernini is on the left, while Borromini was entrusted with the smaller one on the right and shows his passion for curved lines which would be a constant feature of his work. In the Galleria Barberini you will find words by Caravaggio, Tintoretto, Bronzino and more, all attesting to the wealth and power of the Barberini family.

After visiting the museum, exit the palazzo grounds, cross the Via della Quattro Fontane and enter the Via Rosella.

This small, relatively tranquil Roman side street will lead to the Via Traforo, which we will patiently try to cross.

After dodging the zooming herd of motorini and automobiles, head into the small piazza and go down the left street Via Arcone. This lead to Via Lavatore, but before we go any further, would anyone like some gelato from the best ice cream parlor in Rome? If so, take a right onto Via della Panetteria where you will find:

San Crispino *(# 42).* Arguably Rome's best gelateria. The ice cream is made with natural ingredients and no dyes, which means some of the colors of the flavors don't appear as you would imagine. But oh do they taste good.

*After this obligatory gelato stop (you need at least one each day), make your way back down the Via Lavatore and take a right. As you head further along the Via Lavatore you'll notice the crowds start to thicken. That's because we are about to come to the world-famous, the impressive (drum roll please), the incomparable… **Trevi Fountain**.*

On the left before you get to Trevi is the church of **Saints Vincenzo and Anastasio**. This church was bequeathed by the pope to the Orthodox church as part of the pope's on-going efforts to bring the Orthodox and Catholic churches closer together. But why dally in yet another church when to the right is the Trevi Fountain.

Without a doubt this is the most famous fountain in all of Rome, a true masterpiece both of sculpture and of architecture. Begun by Bernini and completed over a hundred years later by Nicola Salvi between 1732 and 1751. The Trevi fountain is at the end of the Aqua Virgo, an aqueduct constructed in 19 BCE, which brings water all the way from the Salone Springs around 20km from Rome, and supplies most of the fountains in the historic center of Rome with water. Remember to come back at night, because when the fountain is all lit up it is truly a sight to behold.

Once you've taken in the whole scene, and tossing the requisite coin over your left shoulder into the fountain to ensure, as legend has it, that you will return to Rome, head around the left side of the fountain as you face it to Via Crocifero.

When this road turns into the Via Sabini it arrives at the newly renovated **Galleria Alberto Sordi**. Head into the galleria, savor the elegance, stop for a drink, grab a bite to eat or do some shopping. Refined Italian gallerias such as this, including those in Naples and Milan, were the inspiration for the creation of bland American-style malls.

After realizing how far from the tree the acorn has sprouted, head out of the Galleria onto the Via del Corso. Dodge more motorbikes and cars and head into the **Piazza Colonna**. Considered by Romans to be the center of the city, this piazza's main feature is the Colonna Antonina erected by

Marcus Aurelius to celebrate his victories in Armenia, Persia and Germany almost 2000 years ago. In 1589 Sixtus V restored the column and Christianized it by adding the statue of St. Paul to the top. The reliefs are a vivid account of ancient Roman life. Take the time to admire them. Binoculars would come in handy.

The column is surrounded by a series of elegant buildings, one of which contains an awesome soccer store:

AS Roma Store *(#360, www.asromastore.it).* Here you can find all sorts of official soccer merchandise for one of Rome's two top-level soccer teams, AS Roma. This is a great place to get a unique keepsake or gift. You can also get tickets for soccer games here.

Right now, we're going to take a little detour on our way to the Pantheon so we can visit my favorite enoteca in all of Rome, Vini e Buffet. If it is not meal time, remember to come back here later.

First exit the AS Roma Store, bear to your left and cross the Piazza Colonna. Enter the Piazza di Monte Citorio. On the right is that rear of Italy's Parliament building. Take the street on the other side of the Parliament, Via della Missione, descend the steps and walk through the Piazza del Parliamento to the Via di Campo Marzio. Follow this to the Piazza del Toretta and turn left.

At the end of this small piazza, on the left, is: **Vini e Buffet** *(Vicolo del Toretta #100).* A characteristic Roman eatery with friendly staff, excellent food and an extensive wine list.

From here head back to the Via di Campo Marzio and take a right. Return to the Piazza del Parliamento and take a right on the Via Prefetti. Follow this through the Piazza Firenze to the Via Ascanio.

You are getting deeper and deeper into Rome's centro storico, its old historic district. This is one of the best places to get a feel for authentic Roman life. And it is where you will find, on the the Via della Scrofa, some great little food stores including:

Volpetti *(# 31/33).* You should come here the day before your flight and stock up on Parmiggiano Reggiano to bring back with you. Ask them to vacuum seal it (mettere sotto vuoto) so it retains its freshness. Hard cheeses such as Parmiggiano will get through customs. Salami, other meats, and soft cheeses will not. If Volpetti has some dried porcini mushrooms, pick some of those up as well. And also grab some specialty pasta so that when you get home you can whip up a tasty Roman meal with actual Roman ingredients.

Once you've devoured what this store have to offer, exit and turn left on the Via della Scrofa. Go to the Via Stelleta and take a left.

On this street on the right hand side is a jumbled, chaotic, but ever so rewarding little box and stationery store:

Scatole *(# 27).* Here you will find similar products offered at the nearby Il Papiro except that here they will generally be half the price.

From here keep following the Via Stelleta to the Piazza Campo Marzio. Take a right, then go the Via Maddalena, take another right and head down the road to the Pantheon.

The **Pantheon** is one of the oldest in Rome. Built in 27

PUB TIP

Black Duke
Via Maddelena, 29
Tel. 06/6830-0381

One of Rome's many Irish-style pubs. If you're wondering why there are so many Irish pubs in Rome, about ten years ago Guinness put together an impressive business plan to increase their stagnant sales – and it worked. Guinness products are sold exclusively in these pubs. Since that time an Irish bar sponsored by Guinness opens every five days somewhere in the world. As a result, Guinness' sales are skyrocketing.

BCE as a Roman temple and later consecrated as a Catholic Church, the monumental porch originally faced a rectangular colonnaded temple courtyard and now fronts the smaller Piazza della Rotonda with its tranquil fountain. Through the huge bronze doors is a single circular room above which rises the 141-foot hemispherical dome that is even larger than the cupola of St. Peter's. Most of the natural light enters through an oculus at the center of the dome. As does inclement weather.

For centuries this was the most expansive unsupported dome in the world. Brunelleschi used it as a model for his magnificent dome over the Duomo in Florence. Opposite the door is a recessed semicircular apse, and on each side are three additional recesses, alternately rectangular and semicircular, separated from the space under the dome by paired monolithic columns. These spaces are filled with a variety of tombs, including that of the world-renowned artist **Raphael** (died 1520).

Our next stop is a church behind and to the left of the Pantheon called Santa Maria Sopra Minerva. The site of the present basilica originally hosted a temple to Minerva, built by Pompey the Great around 50 BCE. It was amidst the ruins of that temple that Pope Zacharias (741-752) built the first church located here. That structure has since disappeared, but the present building owes its existence to the Dominican Friars who received the property from Pope Alexander IV (1254-1261) and made the church and adjoining monastery their headquarters for centuries.

Besides architecture, there are many tombs to be seen in this church. The most important is that of **St. Catherine of Siena** (1347-1380), whose body lies beneath the main altar (her head is in Siena). Then there is Fra Giovanni of Fiesole (1387-1455), known in art history as **Beato Angelico**, who died in the adjoining monastery. His tomb is located in the Frangipane Chapel to the left of the altar choir. This pious Dominican monk was also one of the most renowned painters of the late Middle Ages and early Renaissance. Two of the Renaissance's most powerful popes, **Leo X** (Giovanni de Medici, 1513-1521) and **Clement VII** (Giulio de Medici, 1523-1534), are buried in the choir area behind the altar. Then, from the left wall of the Carafa Chapel, to the right of the altar, scowls the funerary statue of **Paul IV** (1555-1559), the Great Inquisitor of Rome's Counter-Reformation.

Finally, located to the left of the altar is *Christ Carrying the Cross* created by Michelangelo in 1521. Nearby, is one of

Rome's oldest and best artisan chocolate shops.

To get there leave the church of SM Sopra Minerva, take a left down the Via San Chiara, and snake your way along this road to the Piazza Collegio Romano. The store will be on the left as you enter the piazza.

Moriando & Gariglio *(Via del Pie di Marmo #21)*. Here you will find some delicious hand made chocolates, perfect snacks for later, or a great gift to have wrapped to bring home with you.

To end this tour, head over to the Galleria Doria-Pamphili *(Piazza del Collegio Romano, 2. Web: www.doriapamphilj.it)* where you will find a former private home that is now a fantastic museum containing an incredible art collection and a number of apartments dolled up with exquisite furnishings. For only 8 Euros, you will enter a bygone era of wealth, power and intrigue. This is more than an art museum, it is literally a step back in time. Highly recommended.

Centro Storico Walk 2

Featured Sights: *Pantheon, Museo Altemps, Piazza Navona, Campo dei Fiori, Piazza Farnese, Palazzo Farnese*

We'll be starting this walking tour near where we ended the last one, at the Pantheon. If you're in need of sustenance the Piazza della Rotunda is filled with cafes from which to choose, including a McDonald's. There's also a supermarket (Spar) nearby at Via Giustiniani #18 if you want to pick up a bottle of water or some snacks for the walk.

From the Pantheon, take the Via del Pantheon, which turns into the Via della Maddalena, to Via delle Copelle and turn left.

As you pass through Via Sant'Agostinare stop in the **Basilica di Sant'Apollinare**. The main attraction in this church is the remains of Saint

74 ROME MADE EASY

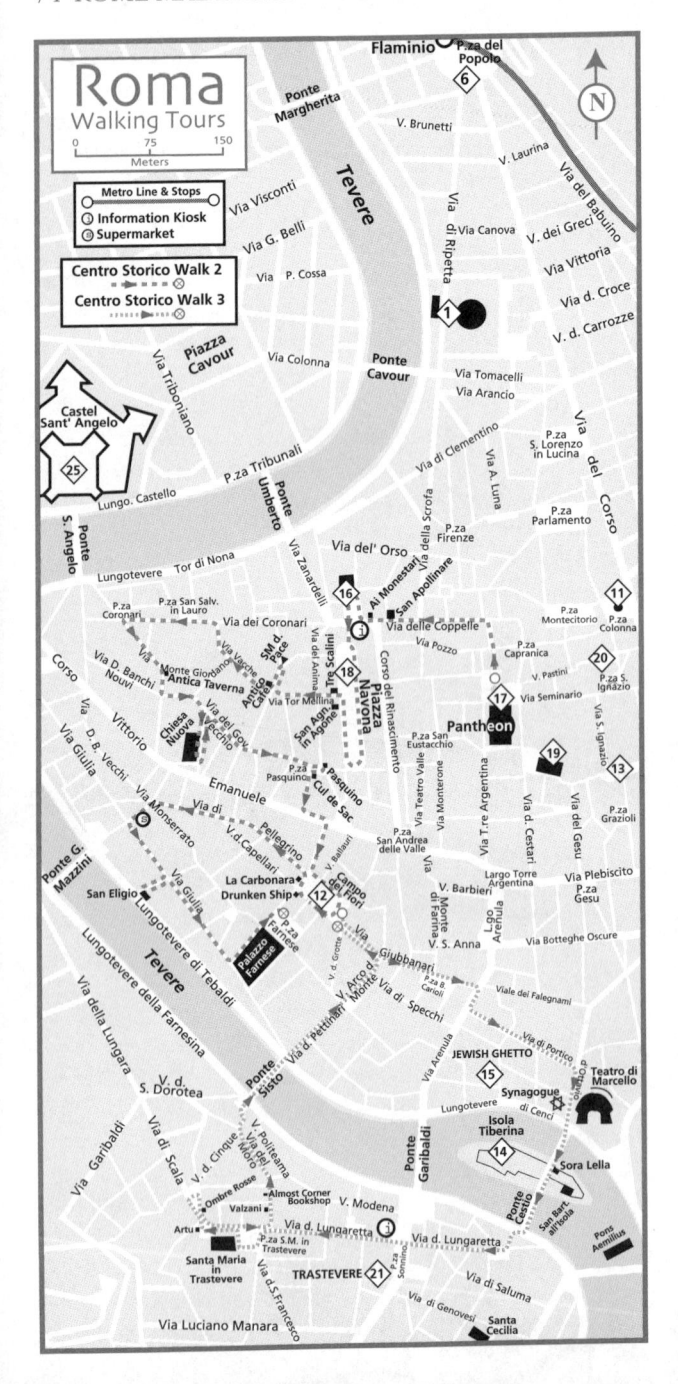

Monica. Though not artistically thrilling, how often are we able to be so close to a saint.

From here continue down Via Sant'Agostinare to Piazza Cinque Lune where you'll find the wonderful little store:

Ai Monesteri *(Corso Rinascimento 72).* Here you will find all sorts of products made with loving care by monks and nuns throughout Italy including jams, jellies, liqueurs, scents, soaps and more. (Building currently being renovated.)

Around the corner to the right is the **Museo Altemps** *(Piazza Sant'Appolinare 48).* Visit here to see how the ancient Roman aristocracy lived. Filled with a legendary collection of ancient statues of pagan gods, fauns, satyrs, nymphs, athletes and warriors. This is a one of a kind museum in a unique palazzo evoking the ambiance of an ancient era.

When finished here, exit straight ahead, cross the piazza and traverse the busy street before entering the next destination: Piazza Navona.

Take some time to notice the brief excavation to the right of the entry. This clearly shows the remnants of the foundation for the **Circus Domitianus** that was inaugurated in 81 CE and which now gives form and shape to Piazza Navona. It also gives us an insight into how, over the ages, silt, dirt, dust and refuse have all piled on top of one another to raise the level of Rome to its current level.

Now let's enter one of Rome's most famous squares. At 240 meters long and 65 wide the Piazza Navona preserves the dimensions of an ancient track where gladiators fought, horses raced, and at times naval battles were contested after the arena had been flooded.

In the center of the piazza is Bernini's spectacular **Fontana dei Fiumi** erected in 1651. It features a central rocky structure that supports an obelisk surrounded by four giant statues representing the Nile, the Danube, the Ganges, and the Rio della Plata.

Nearby, on the western side of the piazza stands the church of **Sant'Agnese in Agone**. It was on this location that myth tells us Saint Agnese had her clothes ripped off prior to her execution, but was then miraculously covered by a prodigious growth of her hair to preserve her saintly modesty. Though her purity was preserved her life was lost, as she was executed anyway. Back in the real world, the church was completed by Francesco Borromini around 1652.

Take note of one of the statues on Bernini's *Fontana dei Fiumi* and how it is covering his face in disgust as it looks away from Borromini's church. Some speculate that this is a result of the intense rivalry between the two artists. Others say it is because the church was built on the site of a former brothel. You make the call.

At the northern end is the *Fontana di Nettuno*, the basin of which was carved by Giacomo della Porta in 1546. And at the southern end, the *Fontana del Moro* was designed by Bernini and features the statue of a Moor fighting with a dolphin. If you're tired or want some sustenance, try a world famous café:

Tre Scalini *(# 28, Web: www.paginegialle.it/trescalini).* An ideal spot to absorb the beauty of the piazza and grab an ice cream cone, coffee, or other snack.

Now we are going to take a short stroll through one of Rome's most characteristic local neighborhoods. Filled with twisting, winding cobblestone streets, here you will find haven from the hordes of tourists that thunder through the rest of Rome. Off the beaten path, and filled with some great cafes, restaurants, as well as a sense of ancient peace and serenity, to many this area is the true heart of Rome.

From the Tre Scalini head down the Via Sant' Agnese in Agone, which turns into the Via Tor Mellina then the Via della Pace. At the corner of the Via della Pace is:

Antico Caffe della Pace *(# 3-7).* Beautifully vine covered, this is a great place to stop for sustenance and to savor the ambiance of this area.

After a brief respite, as you face the café, go down the angled Via della Pace to the right to the beautiful **Santa Maria della Pace**. Known mainly for its Raphael fresco of the four sybils, each of whom holds a scroll upon which is transcribed a revelation about the end of the world.

After your church visit, head back to the café, and turn right. Follow this leg of the Via della Pace to the Via Vacche which turns into the Via della Vetrina. Take a left at Via dei Coronari, go past the Piazza di S. Salvatore in Lauro and head to Piazza Coronari.

There are antique stores galore in this section, so feel free to explore. Also, take the time to head down side streets. The beauty of this section of the walking tour is in the overall ambiance of the whole area.

Take a left onto Via Panico, which turns into Via Monte Giordano. As it bears to the left at the Antica Taverna (#12) take a right onto the teeny tiny Vicolo dell'Avica that leads to the Via del Governo Vecchio. Take a left onto this street then an immediate right onto the Via Chiesa Nuova. Follow this to the Chiesa Nuova.

Though called the new church, **Chiesa Nuova** was finished in 1605 on the sight of a previous church, Santa Maria in Vallicella. This is a typical counter reformation style church generally typified by a double-storied triple part façade with scrolls. The interior is of one huge hall-like nave, with a shallow apse and lateral chapels. The inside also contains a lush display of stucco and gold whirls of painted angels and spiraling clouds, and swirls of blue and crimson draperies. All created by Pietro da Cortona (Pietro Berrettini), seventeenth-century Rome's most sought-after ceiling painter, his frescoed vaults over the nave (St. Philip's Vision of our Lady and the Falling Beam), cupola (Trinity in Glory), and apse (Assumption of the Virgin) are bright, dramatic and immediately appealing.

Apart from these frescoes, the Chiesa Nuova's greatest treasures are three early (1607-1608) paintings by **Peter Paul Rubens**: over the main altar, "Virgin, Child, and Angels," and on either side, "St. Gregory the Great with SS. Maurus and Papius," and "St. Domitilla with SS. Nereus and Achilleus."

When you leave the church, take a left back up the Via Chiesa Nuova to the Via del Governo Vecchio. Take a right. This will lead you to the Piazza Pasquino.

At the far end of this piazza is the *Pasquino*, one of Rome's "talking" statues. In centuries past, when public and open discourse of rulers was not advised, this statue was one of those in Rome where satirical comments were clandestinely attached in the dead of night by political commentators who wanted to share their ideas with the rest of the populace. Frowned on by the authorities, the practice was tacitly accepted to allow the disgruntled some outlet for their frustration.

If you're hungry, in the Piazza Pasquino can be found a superb place to grab a bite to eat:

Cul de Sac *(# 73)* A superb wine bar with light snacks and an extensive wine list.

*When done here, take a left our of Cul de Sac, take a left onto the Via Leutari to the busy Via Vittorio Emanuele II. Cross the street, go to your left, and take a right into the Piazza della Cancelleria which leads to the popular **Campo dei Fiori**.*

There is a market here every morning except Monday from around 6:00am until 1:00pm where you can get all sort of fresh produce, assorted foods, and dry goods. This piazza is also a great place to come at night for dinner and drinks:

La Carbonara *(#23)*. Though a little touristy when the accordion player comes around, this place serves great food including the best spaghetti alla vongole verace I've ever had.

The Drunken Ship *(# 20/21, www.drunkenship.com)*. American owner Regan Smith has created a wild and raucous US style bar in one of Rome's oldest piazzas. It has hopping music, upbeat crowds, tasty light food, draft beer and bilingual and beautiful waitresses. This is the place to come to meet fellow travelers, foreigners living in Rome, or locals and party the night away.

When done here, take the street that was on the right as you entered the piazza, the Via del Pellegrino.

This entire area, from the Campo dei Fiori towards St. Peters and bordered by the Lungotevere and Corso Vittorio Emanuele is filled with antiques store, artisan work shops, and more. This is another great place to explore, so please feel free to deviate from the walking tour and head down side streets.

Follow the Via San Pellegrino as it curves around to the Vicolo della Moretta and take a left. Follow this to the Via Giulia and take a left.

The Via Giulia slices through Rome's historic district as a wide, straight avenue. It replaced a rabbit-warren of alleys, where gangs of brigands and pickpockets would prey upon pilgrims. Today this area is one of the city's poshest addresses.

Note the archway at the end of Via Giulia bedecked with ivy. More than a great spot for a photo op, it is also a history lesson. This archway used to be a part of a private bridge that once spanned the entire Tiber River linking the Palazzo Farnesina on the other side with the Palazzo Farnese on this side. The Farnese family had some pull in centuries past.

On a side trip from the Via Giulia, duck to the right down the Vicolo Sant' Eligio to see the church of Sant' Eligio degli Orefici.

This church was Raphael's first architectural project and is often considered one of the purest expressions of Renaissance architecture (1516). A cupola crowns this small beautiful structure, laid out in an austere Greek cross plan. Though the church is damp, somewhat gloomy, heavily restored and rarely open, it is nonetheless one of the area's hidden treasures. One which most tourists miss.

After visiting this church, head back to the Via Giulia, turn right and take it to the Via Farnese, which is at the ivy covered arch way. Take a left onto the Via Farnese.

The large building on your right is the **Palazzo Farnese**, partially designed by Michelangelo, and is now the French Embassy. At the end of this road is the **Piazza Farnese**. This walking tour is now ended but please feel free to take some time wandering around this area. There are artisan workshops to discover and great local cafes and restaurants to stumble upon. The next walking tour commences in the Campo dei Fiori, which is through one of the three streets in front of the Palazzo Farnese.

Centro Storico Walk 3

Featured Sights: *Campo dei Fiori, Jewish Ghetto, Teatro di Marcello, Sinagoga, Isola Tiberina, Trastevere, SM in Trastevere.*

This walk starts near where we ended the last one, in the **Campo dei Fiori**. From here go down Via Giubbanaro where you'll find some wonderful little boutiques, food stores, and more. This is a rather eclectic local area and even includes the local party headquarters for the successor to the Italian Community Party.

Follow this street into the Piazza Cairoli and cross the busy Via Arenula on the left side of the piazza. After you cross the street, take a right and go to the Via S. Mario di Pianto and take a left.

Now you are in the **Jewish Ghetto**. Long before any Pope reigned in Rome, another religion thrived here: Judaism. The ancient Jewish quarter is a peaceful, tiny riverside neighborhood with narrow curving street and ocher apartment buildings. It looks much like any other section of Rome until closer inspection reveals Kosher food signs, men in skullcaps and stars of David. Technically the Ghetto ceased to exist in 1846 when its walls were torn down, but the neighborhood that retains its name remains home to Europe's oldest and proudest Jewish community.

As you get to the Via Portico d'Ottavio, if you look closely, you will see Roman columns, bas reliefs, arches and more set in the surrounding modern buildings. A pastiche of old and new offers itself as a testament to the age of this neighborhood. Just before this street bends to the right, on the left hand side is a superb pasty shop:

Dolceroma *(#20b)*. Here you can find chocolate chip cookies, chocolate fudge brownies, and sorts of tasty morsels. A highly recommended place to get some refreshment.

At the angle of the Via Portico d'Ottavia on the left hand side is the **Teatro di Marcello** *(www.roma2000.it/zmarce.html)*. Begun by Julius Caesar and eventually dedicated by Augustus Caesar to the memory of his nephew and son-in-law Marcellus. This was one of greatest theaters in ancient Rome, able to hold around 15,000 spectators. Regrettably, it was used as a source of building materials after the fall of Rome, then as a Medieval fort. Eventually it was transformed into a sumptuous Renaissance palazzo for the noble Savelli family. This metamorphoses is still evident by the existence of large glassed windows above the amalgamation of the high arches of the ancient theater and Medieval fortified walls. Modern additions such as electricity and plumbing continue to make the Renaissance palace habitable.

Wander down into the excavation site to be able to see the windows above the ruins. Imagine living in an old Roman amphitheater? That is what Rome is all about. Living in this city means living surrounded by history. The Teatro di Marcello is simply a more pronounced example of that reality.

In the nearby **synagogue museum** *(Lungotevere de Cenci)* you will find a plan of the original ghetto, as well as artifacts from the 17th century Jewish communit .

*Now let's cross the Ponte Fabricio onto the **Isola Tiberina**, a great place to take a breather from the hectic pace of Roman life.*

This island was once the dumping ground for dead and sick slaves. At that time, around the 3rd century BCE, there was also a cult of healing located here. Now a hospital takes up most of the island giving credence to the phrase, "What's past is only prologue."

One of the churches here, S**an Bartolomeo all'Isola** was built in the 12th century and is now something of an architectural pastiche with a Baroque facade, a Romanesque bell tower, 16 ancient Roman columns, and avant-garde 20th-century stained glass windows. Another sight to see, visible south of the Isola Tiberina is the remains of the ancient **Pons Aemilius**.

If hungry or thirsty, stop at the single café, **Caffeteria** *(#18),* on the island and grab a seat at one of the outdoor tables in the piazza. If in need of a sit down meal, there is superb restaurant on the island:

Sora Lella *(Via di Ponte Quattro Capi 16.).* Great food and atmosphere in a truly unique location.

Take the time to wander around the island by the water by accessing the set of stairs to the left of the hospital entrance. This is a spot the vast majority of tourists never get to.

*Now cross the Ponte Cestio and enter **Trastevere**, which literally means "across the river."*

Until recently Trastevere was one of the poorest sections of Rome, but has rapidly become gentrified. These changes have not altered the area's charm. You'll still find interesting shops and boutiques, and plenty of excellent restaurants among the small narrow streets and piazzette (small squares). The maze of streets is a fun place to wander.

To get here, first cross the busy Lungotevere, then go down a small flight of steps and take a right. Go through the Piazza in Piscinula to the Via della Lungaretta. Along the way are restaurants, cafes, and newly emerging upscale shops. Follow this street across the busy Viale Trastevere all the way to Piazza Santa Maria in Trastevere.

Here you'll find one of Rome's earliest basilicas and the first to be dedicated to the Virgin Mary – **Santa Maria in Trastevere**.

Built in the 4th century and remodeled between 1130-1143, It is best known for its prized mosaics, especially the 12th and 13th century representation of the Madonna which adorns the facade of the church. The Romanesque bell-tower was built in the 12th century.

After you exit the church, take a left and go around the corner and pass into an area colloquially known by some as "Little America."

Just as we have Chinatowns and Little Italy's in the US, Rome has its own gathering spot for North Americans. The reason it is here is twofold. First, this is where the English language movie theater, **Il Pasquino**, is located. Second, an American university, John Cabot, is nearby. As a result, you can find a series of cafes that mimic the look and feel of American style bars.

This is where the American ex-pat community comes for a movie and dinner and drinks afterwards. Two places to consider are:

Ombre Rosse *(Piazza Sant'Egidio 12)*. Great atmosphere, drinks, and light meals.

Artu *(Largo MD Fumasoni Biondi 5)*. Situated in a deconsecrated chapel, what better atmosphere to revere the pagan god of wine and wild entertainment, Bacchus.

This entire area is another to take the time to head down side streets and explore. Trastevere is a maze of tiny streets, many of which contain unique sights, enticing aromas, and memories to bring home with you.

When you've seen enough, go back into and across the Piazza SM Maria in Trastevere to the street you came down to get here, Via della Lungaretta. As you exit the piazza, take the first left onto Via del Moro. On the left a little way down will be:

Pasticceria Valzani *(# 37)*. This is, in my opinion, one of the best and most authentically local pasty shops in Rome. With delectable cookies, chocolates, and cakes, you can satisfy a serious sweet tooth here.

Almost Corner Bookshop *(#45)*. Here you find a jumble of English language books if you've finished the one you are currently reading.

If you keep following Via del Moro you will arrive at the Piazzale Trilussa on the Tiber River. Cross the busy Lungotevere on this side and access the pedestrian bridge, Ponte Sisto. On the other side, cross the Lungotevere there, follow the Via Pettinari to the Via Arco dei Monti. At its end, take a left onto the Via Gubbonari.

The Campo dei Fiori is just ahead. Stop here for some rest and refreshment. This walking tour is ended. I hope these small tours have offered you a glimpse into the heart and soul of this wonderful city of Rome.

ant
3. MISCELLANY

Accommodations

Every hotel in Italy earns a specific rating from the Italian Tourist Board. This has more to do with the amenities offered, than the price charged. The following list describes the amenities offered by each rating, as well as a possible price charged.

*****Five star, deluxe hotel: Professional service, high-level restaurant, immaculate large rooms and bathrooms with air conditioning, satellite TV, mini-bar, room service, laundry service, and every convenience you could imagine to make you feel like a king or queen. Price: upwards of $250-300 per night.

****Four star hotel: Professional service, most have a restaurant, clean rooms some not so large, air conditioning, TV, mini-bar, room service, laundry service and maybe a few more North American-style amenities. Price: between $200-300 per night.

***Three star hotel: a little less professional service, most do not have room service, air conditioning, TV and mini bar, but the rooms can be small as can the bathrooms. Price: between $150-250 per night.

**Two star hotel: Usually a family run place, some not so immaculate as higher rated hotels. Generally you'll only find a telephone in the room, but probably not air conditioning. Many but not all the rooms will have bathrooms in the room. Hardly any amenities, just a place to lay your head. Price: between $100-200 per night.

ROME'S BEST HOTELS

TWO STARS

Merano, *Via Vittorio Veneto 155, Tel. 06/482-1796, Fax 06/482-1810. Web: www.guestinitaly.com/hotels/rome/r002.htm.* All credit cards accepted. 30 rooms 28 with bath. Single without bath €50-60; Single €60-70; Double without bath €70-90; Double €90-120.

Parlamento, *Via delle Convertite 5, Tel. 06/6992-1000, Fax 06/679-2082. Email: hotelparlamento@libero.it. Web: www.hotelparlamento.it.* All credit cards accepted. 22 rooms, 19 with bath. Single without bath €65. Single €70-120. Double €90-160. Breakfast included.

THREE STARS

Internazionale, *Via Sistina 79, Tel. 06/6994-1823, Fax 06/678-4764. Email: info@hotelinternazionale.com. Web: hotelinternazionale.com.* All credit cards accepted. 42 rooms. Single €150-180; Double €220-240; Extra bed €55. Buffet breakfast included.

Locarno, *Via della Penna 22, Tel. 06/361-0841, Fax 06/321-5249. Email: info@hotellocarno.com. Web: www.hotellocarno.com.* All credit cards accepted. 38 rooms. Single €130; Double €200-210; Suite €310-510. Breakfast included.

Modigliani, *Via della Purificazione 42, Tel. 06/4281-5226, Email: info@hotelmodigliani.com, Web: www.hotelmodigliani.com.* 28 rooms. Single €120-160; Double €160-200. All credit cards accepted.

Scalinata di Spagna, *Piazza Trinita Dei Monte 17, Tel. 06/679-3006 and 06/679-0896, Fax 06/684-0598. Email: info@hotelscalinata.com. Web: www.hotelscalinata.com.* All credit cards accepted. 16 rooms all with baths. Single €150-310; Double €160-360. Breakfast included.

ROME'S BEST HOTELS

Venezia, *Via Varese 18, Tel. 06/445-7101, Fax 06/495-7687. Email: info@hotelvenezia.com. Web: www.hotelvenezia.com.* Credit cards accepted. 61 rooms. Single €180-190; Double €200. Generous buffet breakfast included.

FOUR STARS

Barocco, *Piazza Barberini 9 (entrance on Via della Purificazione 4), Tel. 06/487-2001/2/3, 487-2005, Fax 06/485-994. Email: hotelbarocco@holelbarocco.it. Web: www.hotelbarocco.com.* 37 rooms. Single €170-220; Double €250-330. Breakfast included. All credit cards accepted.

Mecanate Palace, *Via Carlo Alberto 3, Tel. 06/4470-2024, Fax 06/446-1354. Email: info@mecenatepalace.com. Web: www.mecenatepalace.com.* All credit cards accepted. 62 rooms. Single €260-320; Double €370. Breakfast included.

FIVE STARS

Eden, *Via Ludovisi, 49, Tel. 06/474-3551, Fax 06/482-1584. Email: reservations@hotel-eden.it. Web: www.hotel-eden.it.* 100 rooms. Single €440-460; Double €650-750, Suites €1,800-3,400. Continental breakfast is €14 extra, buffet breakfast is €20.

Hassler, *Piazza Trinita Dei Monti 6, Tel. 06/699-340, Fax 06/678-2651. Email: info@hotelhasslerroma.com. Web: www.hotelhasslerroma.com.* All credit cards accepted. 80 rooms. Single €430-460; Double €520-790. Suites €1,800-3,200. Continental breakfast €23 extra. Buffet breakfast €35 extra.

***One star hotel**: Here you usually get a small room with a bed, sometimes you have to share the rooms with other travelers. The bathroom is usually in the hall. No air conditioning, no telephone in the room, just a room with bed. These are what used to be the low-end pensiones. Definitely for budget travelers. Price: between $50-100 per night.

Be aware that hotels in Rome will be on the expensive side. Also, don't be surprised by hotel taxes, additional charges, and requests for payment for extras, such as air conditioning that make your bill larger than expected. Sometimes these taxes/service charges are included in room rates but you should check upon arrival or when you make your reservation. Remember to save receipts from hotels and car rentals, as 15% to 20% of the value-added taxes (VAT) on these services may be refunded if you are a non-resident. For more information, Tax-Free Shopping section below.

Making Reservations

It is highly recommended to fax or email the hotel(s) of your choice inquiring about availability for the dates you are interested in, as well as the rate for those dates. Since most Italians who run hotels know enough English to communicate effectively, it is possible to write your fax or e-mail in English.

When writing the dates you want to reserve, make sure you spell out the month, since here in America we transpose the month and day in numeric dates. For example, in the US January 10, 2005 would appear numerically as 1/10/05. In Europe, it would appear as 10/01/05. See where the confusion could come in? So spell January.

Expect a reply to your communication within a few days. If you do not get a reply, send another message. Sometimes faxes or emails get lost on the night shift. To book your room you will generally need to send the hotel a credit card number with expiration date in a reply communication. This will ensure that you show up. So if you have to cancel your trip for whatever reason, make sure you contact the hotel and cancel your room - otherwise you will be charged.

Apartment Rentals

Staying in an apartment can save you a lot of money, especially if you are traveling with other couples. For a week, for a two bedroom apartment, sometimes you can pay only $600-800 for a week. Compared to $250 a night for a three star hotel, that is a steal. And you will have more privacy and will be living more like a local than if you stay in a hotel. The only drawback .... no room service, maid service, or concierge. Some suggested places to contact for apartments are:

At Home Abroad Inc, *Tel. 212/421-9165, Fax: 212/752-1591, Web: www.athomeabroadinc.com*

Villas and Apartments Abroad, *Tel. 212/897-5045, Fax 212/897-5039, Web: www.vaanyc.com*

Homebase Abroad, *Tel. 781545-5112, Fax 781/545-1808, Web: www.homebase-abroad.com*

Airports & Getting Around

Most travelers will arrive at Rome's Fiumicino (Leonardo da Vinci) Airport. You may arrive at Rome's Ciampino airport. The website for both of Rome's airports is: *www.adr.it*.

Getting into Rome

Rome's **Fiumicino** has a dedicated train to whisk you directly to Rome's central train station (**Stazione Termini**). The trip costs €8.5 one way and takes 30 minutes. There are trains every half hour. They start operating from the airport to Termini at 7:38am and end at 10:08pm.

When the train arrives at Termini, you catch a taxi to your hotel from the taxi stand in front of the station. You can also hop on the Metro, which is underneath the station, or take one of the many city buses located outside the front of the building.

If you arrive at Rome's **Ciampino** (which is really only used for flights from European counties), there are dedicated airport buses that leave for the Anagnina Metro Station every half an hour. Buses leave from the airport starting at 6:00am and end at 10:30pm.

The only other option for both airports is taking a Taxi (though beware since these will cost an arm and a leg) or taking an Airport Shuttle. See information above.

Airport Shuttle, *Tel. 06/4201-4507, Web: www.airportshuttle.it, Email: airportshuttle@airportshuttle.it.*

Airport Connection Services, *Tel. 06/338-3221. Web: www.airportconnection.it. Email: airpcnn@tin.it.*

Boat Service on the Tiber

Five river boats now ply the Tiber from the Isola Tiberina to the Olympic Stadium - a distance of eight kilometers - all for only €1 per person. Landing areas are near these bridges: Garibaldi, Sisto, S. Angelo, Cavour, Risorgimento, Duca d'Aosta. The regular service sets off daily from Ponte Garibaldi at 8:50am.

Cruises with tourist commentary leave daily at 10:00am, 11:30am, 3:30pm, and 5:00pm. Tickets cost €10. Dinner cruises leave Ponte S. Angelo at 10:00pm. Tickets cost €43 per person. For information and bookings telephone 06/678-9361, or visit www.battellidiroma.it.

Cars

Please don't bother. Rome's traffic is too chaotic and the public transportation here so good that a car is not necessary at all. But if you do want to rent on for a day trip outside of the city, contact one of the following places:

Avis, *Termini Station, Tel. Tel. 06/413-0812. Web: www.avis.com.*

Hertz, *Via Veneto #156, 06/821-6881 or 06/321-6834. Web: www.hertz.com.*

National/Maggiore, *Car reservations in Italy 1478/67067. Web: www.maggiore.it.*

Buses

Rome is such a large city that, unless you are extremely fit and have a lot of time on your hands, you will want to take some form of public transport to get from one end to the other. One of the easiest and most inexpensive ways to do this is by bus. Newsstands will sell maps that contain the bus routes. You will definitely need to buy one of them if you decide to use the bus.

At each bus stop, called a fermata, there are signs that list all the buses that stop there. These signs also give the streets that the buses will follow along their route so you can check your map to see if this is the bus for you. In conjunction the times listed on the signs indicate when the bus will pass the fermata so you can plan accordingly.

Be aware that riding the bus during rush hour is like becoming a sardine, complete with the odor, so try to avoid the rush hours of 8:00am to 9:00am, 12:30pm to 1:30pm, 3:30 to 4:30pm, and 7:30pm to 8:30pm. Yes, they have added rush hours because of their siesta time in the afternoon and late store closings.

The bus fare costs €1 and lasts for 75 minutes, during which time you can transfer to any other bus but you can only ride the Metro once. Tickets can be bought at any ATAC booth or kiosk and at tobacco shops (tabacchi), newsstands (giornalaio) and vending machines in the Metro stations. When you get on the bus, stamp your ticket in the yellow machines at the front and back of each bus .

Never board the Metro or a bus without a ticket. If you do not have a ticket or have one and do not stamp it, and an inspector catches you, you face an instant €25 fine.

ATAC Bus Tours

There is a no-frills Giro di Roma tour on the silver bus #110 offered by ATAC, the intra-city bus company *(Tel. 06/4695-2252, Web: www.atac.roma.it)*. This three hour circuit of the city leaves from the information booth in the middle of the Piazza Cinquecento in front of the train station daily at 10:30am, 2:00pm, 3:00pm, 5:00pm and 6:00pm, and takes you to over 80 sites of historic and artistic significance, and stops at the most important sights like the Colosseum, Piazza Venezia, St. Peter's, and more.

Cost is only €7.5 and you can pay by credit card. To book a seat on these luxury buses with tour guides and an illustrated guide book call the number above 9:00am and 7:00pm. Or stop by one of the ATAC ticket booths in front of Termini Station.

Bus Passes

If you are staying in Rome for a while or will be using the buses frequently, you can buy one of the following bus tickets at most newsstands, tabacchi, or ATAC booths by the station, and in the Metro. These tickets are:

Daily Ticket (B.I.G.): €5 (Valid for unlimited Metro,

Bus, Trolley and Train with the Commune di Roma which includes going to Ostia but not Fiumicino Airport or Tivoli)

Weekly Ticket (C.I.S.): €16 (Valid for everything under the B.I.G.)

Metro

The Roman Metro *(Web: www.atac.roma.it)* has two lines (Linea A and Linea B) that intersect below Termini station. You'll find these and all other stations marked with sign featuring a prominent white "M" inside a red square. The Metro runs from 5:30am to 11:30pm and gets real crowded during rush hour.

Always be on the lookout for pickpockets. The best way to do that is to put your wallet in your front pants pocket, or buy one of those fanny packs, wear it in front of you, and lock the pouch, so that no unwanted hands cannot get inside.

Though not generally a problem, women may be the recipients of unwanted pats on the derriere. If you do feel hands on you, be sure to push them away and say "Basta" (enough) or "Non toccare" (do not touch) loud enough for others to hear. The Italians are good about coming to the aid of a damsel in distress.

It is best to have a ticket in hand when you head down to the Metro since the machines that dispense tickets are, in true Italian fashion, usually out of service. So, get a ticket at a tabacchi or newsstand before coming to the Metro. These cost €1. Before entering the Metro, you will need to stamp these tickets in the yellow stamp machines at the turnstiles. The ticket is valid for one trip.

See the map on the next page for Rome's Metro stops.

Taxis

Taxis are the best, but also the most expensive, way to get around Rome. They are everywhere so flagging one down is not a problem. However, since taxis are costly I wouldn't rely on them as your main form of transportation. Use them as a last resort, Also, have a map handy when a cabby is taking you somewhere. Since they are on a meter, they sometimes decide to take you on a little longer journey than necessary.

Be aware that if you have your hotel call you a taxi the cab's

MISCELLANY 93

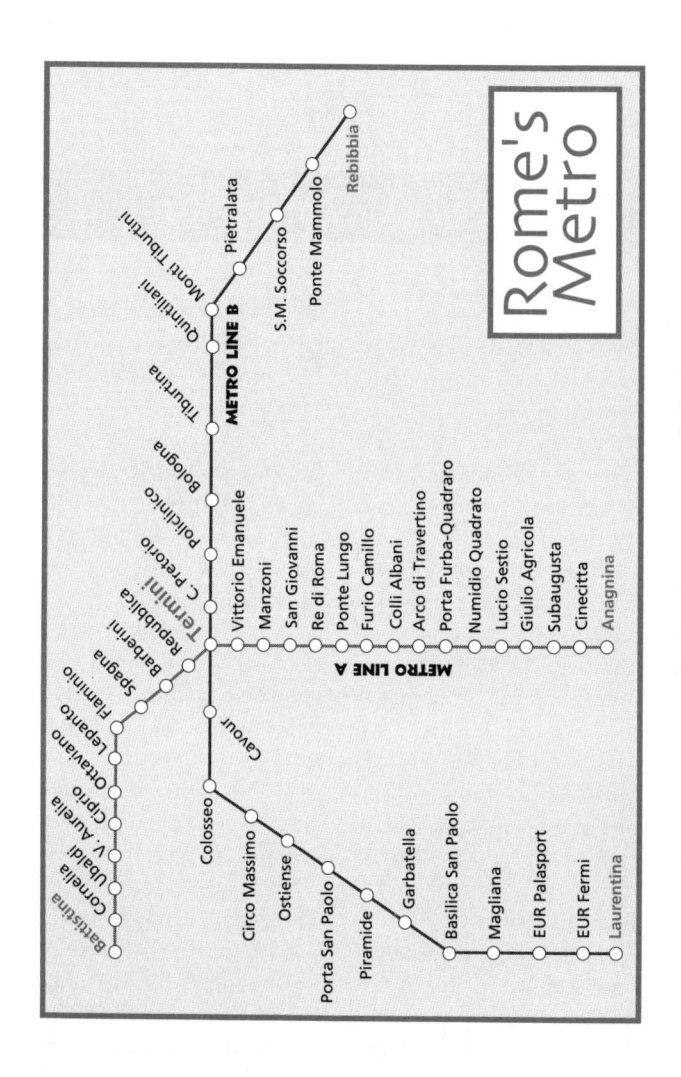

meter starts running when it is summoned, not when it arrives to pick you up. So by the time a cab arrives at your location there will already be a substantial amount on the meter. Also be aware that there will be surcharges at night, for luggage, and on Sundays.

Other Basic Information

Climate & Weather
The climate in Rome is as varied as the country itself, but it never seems to get too harsh. However, in recent years the summers have been rather harsh, though winters have been rather mild. Winter is generally the rainy season, when stream beds that remain empty during much of the year fill to overflowing. Spring and Fall are both very moderate times of year and are my favorite times to visit. However, do bring an umbrella and rain coat just in case.

Business Hours
Stores in Rome are generally open Monday to Friday, 9:00am-1:00pm, reopen at 3:30 or 4:00pm and stay open until 7:30/8:00pm. Some stores in the center of town are now open on Saturday afternoons and Sundays as well. Meal times for lunch are generally 1:00pm to 3:30pm. For dinner 7:30pm until 11:00pm.

Banking & Changing Money
Banks in Rome are generally open Monday through Friday, 8:30am to 1:30pm and from 2:45pm to 4:00pm, and are closed all day Saturday and Sunday and on national holidays. Each bank offers a different rate and exchange fee, as do the Casa di Cambio, smaller exchange shops that are dotted all over the landscape.

These days the way to get the best rate and lowest exchange fee is by using ATM Machines. Called Bancomat machines, one drawback is that you can only withdraw around €300 each day. However, the advantages of using an ATM are that they give you excellent, up-to-date exchange rates that are better than most exchange offices. Also, the transaction fee, a fixed rate of around $2.00, is usually lower than the fees charged by currency exchange places. Another advantage is that you are not constrained by bank or business hours. You can access your money anytime.

That being said, I would strongly suggest bringing some travelers checks with you. Why? If there is a bank strike (and that could happen at any time in Italy), the ATMs won't be filled up with cash and you'd be left without money. Also have a credit card handy just in case as well.

Electricity

If you want to use any electrical device you bring with you, you are going to need a hardware adapter to switch the appliance from a US-style small two-prong to a two- or three-prong Italian plug.

Also, since the standard electric current in Italy is 220v, check before you leave to see if your appliance automatically changes the voltage from 110v to 220v. If it doesn't, you will need to purchase a converter as well. If you can't find adapters or converters at your hardware store or local Radio Shack, you can order them from the Magellan, *www.magellan.com*.

Embassies & Consulates

Australia, *Via Alessandria 205, Tel. 06/852-721, Web: www.australian-embassy.it.*

Canada, *Via GB de Rossi 27, Tel. 06/445-981, Web: http://canadaonline.about.com/library/fed/blfembitaly.htm.*

Great Britain, *Via XX Settembre 80a, Tel. 06/482-5441, Web: www.grbr.it.*

Ireland, *Piazza di Campitelli 3, Tel. 06/697-9121, Web: http://foreignaffairs.gov.ie/embassies/display.asp*

United States, *Via Veneto 199, Tel. 06/46741, Web: www.usembassy.it*

Emergencies

The following numbers should be used in case of emergency:

113 - Police

112 - Caribinieri (the Italian equivalent to the FBI/DEA/CIA/Customs and other national law enforcement agencies)

118 - Ambulance (Red Cross)

115 - Fire

Festivals in Rome

January 1, Candle-lit processional in the Catacombs of Priscilla to mark the martyrdom of the early Christians.

January 5, Last day of the Epiphany Fair in the Piazza Navona. A carnival celebrates the ending.

January 21, Festa di Sant'Agnese. Two lambs are blessed then shorn. Held at Sant'Agnese Fuori le Mura.

March 9, Festa di Santa Francesca Romana. Cars are blessed at the Piazzale del Colosseo near the church of Santa Francesca Romana.

March 19, Festa di San Giuseppe. The statue of the saint is decorated with lamps and placed in the Trionfale Quarter, north of the Vatican. There are food stalls, sporting events and concerts.

April, Festa della Primavera (festival of Spring). The Spanish Steps are festooned with rows upon rows of azaleas.

Good Friday, The Pope leads a candlelit procession at 9:00pm in the Colosseum.

Easter Sunday, Pope gives his annual blessing from his balcony at noon.

April 21, Anniversary of the founding of Rome held in Piazza del Campidoglio with flag waving ceremonies and other pageantry.

May 6, Swearing in of the new guards at the Vatican in St. Peter's square. Anniversary of the sacking of Rome in 1527.

First Sunday in June, Festa della Repubblica involving a military parade centered on the Via dei Fori Imperiali. It's like something you'd see in Moscow during the Cold War.

June 23-24, Festa di San Giovanni. Held in the Piazza di Porta San Giovanni. Traditional roast baby pig and snails sold.

June 29, Festa di San Pietro. Festival of Saint Peter.

July, Tevere Expo involving booths and stalls displaying arts and crafts, with food and wine lined up along the Tiber. At night there are fireworks displays and folk music festivals.

MISCELLANY 97

July & August, Open air opera performances in the Baths of Caracalla.

Early September, Sagra dell'Uva. A harvest festival with reduced price grapes and music provided by performers in period costumes held in the Roman Forum.

December 8, Festa della Madonna Immacolata in Piazza di Spagna. Floral wreaths inlaid around the column of the Madonna and one is placed at the top by firefighters.

Mid-December, Start of the Epiphany Fair in the Piazza Navona. The piazza is filled with food stands, and candy stands. Loads of fun.

December 20-January 10, Many churches display elaborate nativity scenes.

December 25, Pope gives his blessing at noon from his Balcony at St. Peter's. The entire square is packed with people.

December 31, New Year's Eve. Much revelry. At the strike of midnight people start throwing old furniture out their windows into the streets, so be off the streets by that time, or else your headache from the evening's festivities will be much worse.

Public Holidays

Offices and shops in Italy are closed on the dates below, so prepare for virtually everything being closed. Which means stock up on snacks, soda, whatever, because in Rome there is no such thing as a 24 hour 7-11 store.

January 1, New Year's Day

January 6, Epiphany

April 25, Liberation Day (1945)

Easter Monday

May 1, Labor Day

August 15, Ferragosto and Assumption of the Blessed Virgin

November 1, All Saints Day

December 8, Immaculate Conception

December 25/26, Christmas

Internet Access

Easy Internet Cafe, *Via Barberini 2, Tel. 06/42-903-388. Web: www.easyinternetcafe.it. Only €0.80 per hour. The BEST*

place to access the internet in Rome. Tons of computers, professional space, and a Subway shop inside to satisfy your munchies while surfing.

Packing

One suitcase and one carry-on should suffice for a ten day trip. A suitcase with wheels is important. Items to remember, especially if you're traveling in the winter time, is an umbrella, a raincoat, and water-proof shoes. You should also bring a small pack, or knapsack to carry with you on day trips. A money belt is also advised, because of pick pockets.

But most importantly, bring a comfortable pair of walking shoes that you have already broken in. Without these, your trip will be miserable. A light travel iron is not a bad idea if you cannot abide wrinkles; but a more sensible option is to pack wrinkle free clothes. And in the summer, if you want to get into most of the churches, remember to pack long pants or something to cover your legs. Tank tops and halter top type shirts are also not considered appropriate attire in places of worship.

Finally, pack all your personal cosmetic items since, more than likely, they're not available in Italian stores.

Papal Audiences

General audiences with the Pope are held once a week (Wednesday at 11:00am) in Vatican City. To participate in a general audience, get information through the **North American College** *(Via dell'Umita 30, Tel. 06/679-0658, Fax 06/679-1448, Web: www.pnac.org).* Catholics are requested to have a letter of introduction from their parish priest. Ticket pickup is the Tuesday before the Wednesday audience. For attendance at a Papal audience women should dress modestly, with arms and head covered, and dark or subdued colors are requested. Men are asked to wear a tie and a jacket. If you want to see the Pope, but forgot to plan in advance, at noon every Sunday, the Pope addresses the crowds gathered beneath his window in St. Peter's square.

Passport Regulations

A visa is not required for US, Canadian, British, Australian, or New Zealand citizens who are holding a valid passport, unless that person expects to stay in Italy longer than 90 days for study or to seek employment.

MISCELLANY 99

You will need to produce your passport when you check in so a hotel so they can register you with the police. Your passport will most likely be returned that same day. If not, make sure you request it since it is an Italian law that identification papers be carried at all times. If you are concerned about pickpockets, keep your passport in the front pocket of your pants in a small zip lock bag so it won't get moist with perspiration. Or use a fanny pack.

To find out all the information you need to know about applying for a US Passport go to the State Department website: *http://travel.state.gov/passport_services.html*.

For Canadian travelers, visit the Canadian Passport Office website: *www.dfait-maeci.gc.ca/passport/menu.asp*.

For British travelers, visit the U. K. Passport Agency website: *www.ukpa.gov.uk*.

Phrases & Language
Most people working in the hospitality industry will speak English. However, it is respectful not to expect them to. It is polite to at least try and communicate with Italians while in Italy in their own language. The attempt will be much appreciated. At the very least, you can ask them if they speak English by saying, *"Mi scusi, ma parli Inglese?"* (Excuse me, but do you speak English?)

General Phrases
Excuse me, but ....
Mi scusi, ma ....

Thank you
Grazie

Please
Per favore

"Help"
Aiuto (eye-yoo-toh)

Where is the restaurant (name of restaurant)
Dov'é il ristorante_____?
Note: (Dov'é is pronounced "Dove [as in the past tense of dive] -ay")

Where is the hotel (name of hotel)
Dov'é l'hotel _____?

Where is the museum (name of museum)
Dov'é il museo _____?

Travel-Public Transport
Where is the (name of station) metro station?
Dov'é la stazione del Metró _____?

Where can I buy a Metro ticket?
Dove posso comprare un biglietto per il Metro?

How much is the ticket?
Quanto costa il biglietto?

Where is the bus stop for bus number ___.
Dov'é la fermata per il bus numero ___?

Excuse me, but I want to get off.
Mi scusi, ma voglio scendere.

Where can I catch a taxi?
Dov'é posso prendere un taxi?

Hotel
How much is a double for one night/two nights?
Quanto costa una doppia per una notte/due notti?

How much is a single for one night/two nights?
Quanto costa una singola per una notte/due notte?

Where is the Exit/Entrance?
Dov'é l'uscita/l'ingresso?

What time is breakfast?
A che ora é la prima colazione?

Can I get another....for the room?
Posso prendere un altro ... per la camera?

–blanket
coperta

–pillow
cuscino

–bed
letto

–key
ciave

Miscellaneous
Where is the bathroom?
Dov'é il bagno?

What time is it?
Che ore sono?

Sorry, I don't speak Italian.
Mi scusi, ma non parlo italiano.
Where can I get a ticket for ...?
Dove posso prendere un biglietto per ...?

–a soccer game
una partita di calcio

–the theater
il teatro

–the opera
l'opera

Do you speak any English?
Parli un po d'Inglese?

Postal Services - Rome
You can buy stamps at local tobacconists (they are marked outside with a "T") as well as post offices. Mailboxes are colored red, except for the

international ones, which are blue. Any white boxes you see on the sides of buildings are for medical waste. Don't put your postcards in those.

Post offices are open from 8:30am to 2:00pm on weekdays, and 8:30am to noon Saturday. The two exceptions to this rule are: the **Main Post Office** *(Piazza San Silvestro)*, which is open Monday through Friday from 9:00am to 6:00pm, and Saturday from 8:30am to 12:50pm; and the branch at **Stazione Termini** *(Via Terme Diocleziane 30)*, which is open 8:30am-6:00pm Monday-Friday and Saturdays 8:30am-2:00pm.

Postal Services - Vatican

If you want to have your postcards mailed by the Vatican with one of their stamps, go to the **Vatican Post Office** *(Via di Porta Angelica 23, close to Piazza Risorgimento)* which is open 8:30am-6:00pm Monday-Friday and Saturdays 8:30am-11:50am.

Public Restrooms

These are scarcer than flying pigs, even though many were built for the year 2000 celebrations. When in need, there are always McDonalds, or well-heeled restaurants or hotels. Ask for the servizio, toilette, or bagno.

Safety & Avoiding Trouble

Rome is definitely much safer than any American city. You can walk almost anywhere without fear of harm, but that doesn't mean you shouldn't play it safe. Listed below are some simple rules to follow to ensure that nothing bad happens to you while in Rome:

At night, make sure the streets you are strolling along have plenty of other people.

Always have your knapsack or purse flung over the shoulder that is not directly next to the road. Why? There have been cases of Italians on motor bikes snatching purses off pedestrians.

Better yet, have your companion walk on the street side, while you walk on the inside of the sidewalk with the knapsack or purse.

Better still is to buy one of those tummy wallets/fanny packs that goes under your shirt so no one can even be tempted to purse-snatch you.

Always follow basic common sense. If you feel threatened,

scared, or alone, retrace your steps back to a place where there are other people.

Shopping

The main shopping area is near the Spanish Steps, is known as **Il Tridente**, and is a network of streets featuring the Via della Croce in the north to Via Frattina in the south, and Via del Corso in the west to Piazza di Spagna in the east. This area includes the famous Via Condotti.

Romans, like most Italians, prefer to shop in boutiques, and the Via Condotti area has quaint little shops selling everything from shirts to gloves.

Department stores are the exception rather than the rule, and include La Rinascente, STANDA, UPIM, and Coin. Both STANDA and UPIM are designed for the Italian on a budget, while Rinascente and Coin are a little more upscale.

Some good antique shops in Rome can be found in the Via del Babuino and the Via Margutta. Other such shops can be found on the Via dei Coronari, and the Via Giulia. And don't forget to check out the Porta Portese Sunday market in Trastevere (open 6:30am-2:30pm).

TAX-FREE SHOPPING

Italian law entitles all non-European Union residents to a **VAT** (IVA) tax refund with a minimum purchase exceeding €150. Ask for an invoice (fattura in Italian) or a Tax-Free Check when completing a purchase. This includes hotels.

Direct refunds are offered at major airports by the three major tax free services, Cashback, Global Refund Italia, Tax-Free for Tourists, plus others. You can easily save hundreds of dollars doing this.

The best area to visit to find **antiques** is from Piazza Navona and Campo dei Fiori to the tip of the peninsula that points towards St. Peter's. Filled with artisan's stores, creative little shops, this is a great area to get a feel for what authentic Roman life is like, far away from the thundering herd of tourists.

Supermarkets

You can usually find all the food you need at an alimentari, but if you want a wider selection, there are four supermarkets in the center of Rome, marked on the maps with an "S" in a circle. One, **GS**, is in the Metro tunnel system between the Piazza di Spagna and the Via Veneto. Another, **SMA**, is in the Piazza Santa Maria Maggiore near the train station.

A **Despar** supermarket is at Via del Pozzetto 119-124 near the Via del Tritone and Via del Corso. Finally, there is a supermarket near the Pantheon at Via Giustiniani 18-20.

Telephones

Calling Italy: Even when making local calls the area code must be used. To dial Rome from the United States, first dial the international prefix, 011, then the country code, 39, then the city code for Rome, 06, then the number you wish to reach.

Long Distance Calling From Italy: To call the U.S. direct from Italy, dial 001, then the area code and number. Listed below are some of the major telecommunications carriers for North America and their access numbers:

AT&T - *Tel. 172-1011* (a toll free number in Italy) to gain access to an AT&T operator (or English language prompts) for efficient service. You can bill your AT&T calling card, local phone company card, or call direct.

Canada Direct - *Tel. 172-1001* (a toll free number in Italy) and you will be connected to the Canadian telephone network with access to a bilingual operator. You can bill your Calling Card, Call Me™ service, your Hello! Phone Pass or call collect.

MCI - *Tel. 172-1022* (a toll free number in Italy) for MCI's World Phone and to use your MCI credit card or call collect. All done through English speaking MCI operators.

Sprint - *Tel. 172-1877* (a toll free number in Italy) for access to an English speaking Sprint operator who can charge your phone card or make your call collect.

Pay Phones: Most pay phones in Italy only use domestic phone cards (which you can buy in denominations of €2.5, €5 or €7.5) but some use a combination of cards and coins. Buy phone cards at most tabacchi (the stores with the T out in front of them), newsstands, and post offices.

International Phone Cards: An inexpensive option for international calling is to buy an international phone card *(carta telefonica internationale)* which are sold at most tabacchi and newsstands. You can get cards for €10, which have 300 minutes available on them. This translates to about 3 cents a minute, a steal for international calling. These cards can be used in your hotel room or at public phone booths simply by following the directions on the back. Discerning travelers who do not want to spend an arm and a leg to call home generally pick up a phone card.

Please be aware that sometimes you cannot use international phone cards at pay phones. Also sometimes you need a domestic phone card to get the pay phone to work so you can use the international phone card. When in Italy nothing is done just one way. There is a constant need to be flexible here.

Time
Most of the year, Italy is **six hours ahead of Eastern Standard Time** in North America, so if it's noon in New York it's 6:00pm in Rome. Daylight savings time goes into effect each year in Italy usually from the end of March to the end of September.

Tipping
A service charge of 15-18% is usually added to your **hotel** bill, but it is customary to leave a little something for the maid. Whatever you deem sufficient is fine, but _1-2 per day is generally fine. Add a note with the word "Grazie" (Thank You) to let the maid know it's for her.

In **restaurants**, a service charge of around 10% is usually automatically added to all bills. But if you felt the service was good, it is customary to leave a little something extra. There is no set percentage, and a good rule of thumb is to leave whatever change is returned, as long as it is not above 5%.

The same applies in **cafés and bars**. For example, around €0.50 is normal if you're standing at the counter drinking a soda, cappuccino, etc. Leaving change in this manner is also a good way to rid myself of burdensome coins.

Travel Insurance
The beauty of travel insurance is that it covers a wide variety of occurrences, such as trip cancellation or interruption, trip delay/missed con-

nection, itinerary change, accident medical expense, sickness medical expense, baggage and baggage delay, and medical evacuation/repatriation. And to get all that for a week long trip will only cost you $25.

For travel insurance look in your local yellow pages or contact the well-known international organization **Travelex**, *Tel. 800/228-9792, Web: www.travelex-insurance.com/Consumer/Welcome.htmx.*

Tourist Information & Maps
Besides the tourist kiosks dotted around the city, you can buy maps and guide books at most newsstands and bookstores. This may be necessary as the tourist kiosks tend to run out of information fast. Also, the maps given out at the tourist offices and kiosks are not nearly as extensive as is needed when in Rome, especially if you want to use the bus system. The cost for bus maps at newsstands is around €5. A bargain as well as a great keepsake of your trip to Rome.

Water
Tap water is generally safe to drink in Rome. Occasionally you will find signs in public restrooms that read, *Aqua Non Potabile*. This means that the water should not be ingested.

Websites for Rome
The following websites will help you get a feel for this wonderful city:

www.ciaorome.com
www.romecity.it
www.romebuddy.com
www.comune.roma.it

When to Go
Basically, anytime is good time to travel to Rome. The climate doesn't vary greatly, making for a pleasant trip all year round. The busiest tourist season is from May to October, leaving the off-season of spring and autumn as the choice times to have Rome all to yourself.

Some visitors find January and February to be the ideal months to visit in terms of cost and climate. However, my favorites are March and November. Another plus is that during these months, there will be fewer tourists about.

If you come in the summer months, when most tourists visit, Rome will be a crowded place. Be aware also that in August the entire city literally shuts down, as most Romans go on vacation to the beach or in the mountains.

Whenever you visit, I hope this guide has helped you have a truly memorable vacation.

Dining & Nightlife

Dining

Rome is filled with all sorts of different eateries such as ristorante, trattorie, pizzerie, which generally serve up a full complement of pasta, salads, meat dishes and more. Then there are **enoteche** (wine bars) which usually only serve light meals that do not necessitate any heating or cooking such as salads and sandwiches.

A feature on most menus are **piatti del giorno** (daily specials) and **prezzo fisso** (fixed price offerings). The latter can be a good buy if you like the choices and is usually a better deal than ordering a la carte. In all restaurants in Italy there is a universal cover charge, **pane e coperto** (literally "bread and cover"), which is different restaurant to restaurant. This surcharge is tacked on to your bill above and beyond any tip you decide to leave. Therefore if your bill has an extra €5 or so on it, that is the pane e coperto.

On any restaurant check there should also be a statement about whether service is included (**servizio incluso**) or not (**servizio non incluso**). If service is included it is usually 10% of the bill. If you felt the service was good, it is customary to leave between around 5% more for the waiter.

If you have trouble reading the menu, ask your waiter for assistance. Usually waiters speak enough English to help. And in many restaurants there are menus in different languages to help you choose the food you want.

After your meal, you can also find **gelateria** (ice cream shops) offering some of Italy's world famous ice cream. Finally, if you like pastries like I like pastries, you will not want to miss out on Rome's **pasticcerie** (pastry shops).

The eateries listed below are guaranteed to give you a great meal. You can find them featured by name on maps A, B and D in Chapter 1.

La Canonica, *Vicolo dei Piede 13, just off of the Piazza Santa Maria in Trastevere, Tel. 06/580-3845.* Closed Mondays. Major credit cards accepted. Dinner for two €40.

Sora Lella, *Via di Ponte IV Capi 16, Tel. 06/686-1601.* Closed Sundays. Credit cards accepted. Dinner for two €60.

Al Piccolo Arancio, *Vicolo Scandberg 112, Tel. 06/678-6139.* Closed Mondays. Credit cards accepted. Dinner for two €45.

Le Grotte, *Via delle Vite 37. Tel. 06/679-5336.* Credit cards accepted. Dinner for two €35.

La Buca di Ripetta, *Via di Ripetta 36, Tel. 06/321-9391.* Closed Mondays and the whole month of August. No credit cards accepted. Dinner for two €35.

La Carbonara, *Campo dei Fiori 23, Tel. 06/686-4783.*

DINE WITH A VIEW

These are some cafes and restaurants where you can grab a bite to eat, take a load off, and savor a tantalizing view over the rooftops of Rome. Don't forget your camera!

Caffe del Vittoriano, *Piazza Venezia, Tel. 06/699-1718.*

Caffe Capitolino, *Piazzale Caffarelli 4, Tel. 06/678-8821.*

Eden Hotel Roof Top Ristorante, *Via Ludovisi, 49, Tel. 06/474-3551*

Hassler Hotel Restaurant, *Piazza Trinita dei Monti 6, Tel. 06/678-2651*

Risorante Olimpo, *Bernini Bristol Hotel, Piazza Barberini 23, Tel. 06/4201-0469.*

Credit cards accepted. Closed Tuesdays. Dinner for two €45.

Enotecantica, *Via del Croce 76, Tel. 06/679-0896.* Closed Sundays. All credit cards accepted. Meal for two €28.

Vini e Buffet, *Piazza della Torretta 60, Tel 06/687-1445*. Open 12:30pm-2:30pm and 7:30pm to midnight. Closed Sundays. Meal for two €25.

Cavour 313, *Via Cavour 313, Tel. 06/678-5496*. Open 12:30pm-2:30pm and 7:30pm-12:30am. Closed Sundays. Meal for two €25.

Cul de Sac, *Piazza di Pasquino 73, Tel. 06/6880-1094*. Open 12:30pm-3:30pm and 7:00pm-12:30am. Closed Mondays for lunch. Meal for two €25.

Nightlife

Rome is filled with many discos and pubs where you can spend your evening and nights having wild and raucous times. As you can see from my list below, there are quite a few Irish pubs here!

But if you want to do like most of the Romans do for evening and nightly entertainment, seat yourself at a bar/café or restaurant, savor your meal or a few drinks and revel in the beauty that is Rome. Lingering in the evening air while recalling the day's events or planning tomorrow's is a great way to relax, slow down, and adapt to the Italian culture.

There are a few ideal places in Rome where you can do that.

The best is in **Trastevere** at one of the little open air cafés where you can either stay all night sipping a few glasses of wine, or visit after you've had your dinner in one of the restaurants around the piazza. This is definitely *the* best place to go for a night out in Rome.

Another is **Campo dei Fiori**, which also has many cafés and restaurants where you can sit while you watch the life of Rome amble past. Three other great nightspots are the **Piazza Navona**, around the **Pantheon**, and around the **Trevi Fountain** though these last three are more well known. Hence more tourists. If you're after dancing, **Testaccio** is the neighborhood for you (see Alibi below).

Below are some of Rome's best nightspots:

Alexander Platz, *Via Ostia 9, Tel. 06/3974-2171. Membership entry €6*. Rome's best jazz club.

Alibi, *Via di Monte Testaccio 40/44, Tel. 06/574-3448. Free* admission Wed, Thur, and Sun. Fri & Sat €8-13. *Open after 11pm.* An awesome dance club.

Big Mama, *Via San Francesco a Ripa 18, Tel. 06/581-2551. Membership entry €5.* Rome's "House of Blues."

Black Duke, *Via della Maddelena 29, Tel. 06/6830-0381. Open for lunch in the summers. Open until 2:00am all year long, every day.* Well-located Irish style pub.

Drunken Ship, *Campo dei Fiori 20/21, Tel. 06/683-00-535. Open 1:00pm-2:00am.* The best American bar in the best location in Rome.

Radio Londra, *Via di Monte Testaccio, 65B. Tel. 06/575-0044. Open Monday-Friday 10:00pm to 3:00am, and Saturdays until 4:00am.* A great dance club.

Shamrock, *Via del Colosseo 1/c, Tel. 06/679-1729. Open noon to 2:00am.* The place to play darts in Rome. A truly authentic Irish pub.

Trinity College, *Via del Collegio Romano 6, Tel. 06/678-64-72. Open 7:30am to 3:00pm and 8:00pm to 2:00am.* An upscale Irish pub.

INDEX

ACCOMMODATIONS 85-89
Airport Shuttle 90
Airports 89-90
Altar of Augusts 59, 64
Altar of Augustus 10-12
Antiques 77
Appartamento Borgia 34
Arch of Constantine 37
Arch of Septimus Severus 45
Arch of Titus 48
Aurelian Wall 12, 65

BANKING 94
Basilica Emilia 46
Basilica Giulia 46
Basilica Maxentius 48
Baths of Caracalla 37-39
Baths of Diocletian 12-13
Baths of Septimus Severus 49
Bernini 14, 15, 16, 17, 22, 23, 25, 29, 31, 40, 61, 65, 67, 68, 69, 75, 76
Boats 90
Bocca della Verita 41
Bookstores, English Language 66, 67, 83
Borghese Gardens 13
Borromini 15, 23, 68, 76
Buses 90-92

CAFFE GRECO 62
Campidoglio 39
Campo dei Fiori 18-20, 73, 78, 80
Capitoline Hill 39
Capitoline Museums 8, 39
Care Rental 90
Castel Sant'Angelo 8, 36
Catacombs 52-53
Centro Storico 18-26
Changing Money 94
Chiaramonti Museum 33
Chiesa Nuova 77
Chigi Chapel 65
Church of Bones 16-17, 68
Church of Saints Vincenzo and Anastasia 69
Circus Maximus 40-41
Climate 94
Colonna di Marcus Aurelius 18
Colosseum 41-42
Consulates 95
Cryptoporticus 49
Curia 46-47

DOMUS AUGUSTANA 49
Domus Aurea 43-44
Domus Flavia 49
Domus Livia 49
Domus Tiberiana 48-49

EGYPTIAN MUSEUM 34
Electricity 95
Embassies 95

112 ROME MADE EASY

Emergencies 95
English Language Bookstores 66, 67, 83
Etruscan Museum 33-34
Exchanging Money 94

FARNESE GARDENS 48-49
Festivals 96
Flavian Amphitheater 41-42
Fontana dei Fiumi 76
Forum 37-48
Forum of Augustus 43
Forum of Caesar 43

GALLERIA ALBERTO SORDI 69
Galleria Berberini 68
Galleria Borghese 13-14
Galleria Doria Pamphili 20, 67, 73
Gelato 68-69, 71
Gladiators 41-42
Grotte Vaticano 35
Guided Walks 59-84

HADRIAN'S TEMPLE 25
Hadrian's Villa 40, 57
Holidays 97
Hotels 85-89
House of Vestal Virgins 47

ICE CREAM 68-69, 71
Il Tridente 9, 59-67
Imperial Forums 42-43
Information 105
Internet Access 67, 97
Isola Tiberina 20, 80, 81
Itineraries 59-84

JAMES, HENRY 10
Jewish Ghetto 20-21, 80

KEATS 10

LA PIETA 8, 31
Library of the Vatican 34

Little America 82-83
Loggia of Raphael 35
Lord Byron 10

MAUSOLEUM OF AUGUSTUS 10-12, 59, 64
Metro 92-93
Michelangelo 8, 13, 24, 29, 30, 31, 34, 35, 39, 40, 51, 52
Mithraic 50
Museo Altemps 73, 75
Museo della Civilta Romana 53
Museo di Villa Giulia 14
Museo Nazionale delle Terme 12-13

NERO'S GOLDEN HOUSE 43-44
New Museum 40
Nightlife 106-109

OSTIA ANTICA 55-56

PALACE OF THE CONSERVATORI 39-40
Palatine Hill 44, 48-49
Palazzo Altemps 22
Palazzo Barberini 15, 67, 68
Palazzo Farnese 73, 79
Palazzo Farnesina 79
Pantheon 22-23, 67, 73, 71-72
Papal Audiences 98
Passports 98-99
Phrases 99-100
Piazza Barberini 67
Piazza Colonna 67, 69-70
Piazza del Popolo 15-16, 59, 64
Piazza della Rotunda 71
Piazza di Spagna 9, 16, 59, 61
Piazza Farnese 73, 79
Piazza Navona 8, 23-24, 73, 75-76
Piazza San Lorenzo in Lucina 67
Pinacoteca Capitolina 40
Pinacoteca Vaticano 33
Piramide di Gaius Cestius 53

INDEX 113

Pius Clementine Museum 33
Postal Services 100-101
Public Restrooms 62, 101

RAPHAEL 14, 23, 29, 33, 35, 57, 65, 72, 76, 79
Restaurants 106-109
Roman Forum 44-49
Rooms of Raphael 35
Rostra 46
Rubens, Peter Paul 77

SAFETY 101
San Clemente 49-50
San Giovanni in Laterano 50-51
San Pauloa Fuori le Mure 54-55
San Pietro 29-31
San Pietro in Vincoli 51-52
Santa Agnese in Agone 75
Santa Cecilia in Trastevere 26
Santa Maria d'Aracoeli 39
Santa Maria del Popolo 65
Santa Maria della Concezione 16-17, 68
Santa Maria in Cosmedin 41
Santa Maria in Trastevere 25-26, 82
Santa Maria Maggiore 51
Santa Maria Sopra Minerva 24, 67, 72
Santi Ambrogio e Carlo 66
Senatorial Palace 39
Shelley 10
Shopping 102-103
Sistine Chapel 8, 34-35
Smart Car 66
Spanish Steps 10-12, 16, 59, 61
St. John Lateran 50-51
St. Paul's Outside the Walls 54-55
St. Peter's in Chains 51-52
St. Peters 8, 28-31
Statue of Marcus Aurelius 39

Statue of Moses 51
Synagogue 21-22, 80

TAXIS 92, 94
Teatro di Marcello 80, 81
Telephones 103
Tempio di Adriano 25
Temple of Anthony and Faustina 47
Temple of Caesar 47
Temple of Romulus 48
Temple of Saturn 46
The Wedding Cake 52
Tipping 104
Tivoli Gardens 56-57
Tourist Information 105
Trajan's Forum 42-43
Trajan's Market 43
Trastevere 18, 25-26, 82-83
Travel Insurance 104-105
Trevi Fountain 8, 17, 67, 69
Twain, Mark 10

VATICAN 26-36
Vatican City 26-28
Vatican Museums 8, 31-36
Via Condotti 59, 62, 67
Via del Corso 18, 59, 62, 63, 66, 69
Via della Croce 63
Via delle Carrozze 62, 63
Via Giulia 79
Via Veneto 10-12, 13, 17-18
Villa Adriano 40, 57
Villa d'Este 57
Villa Gregoriana 57
Vittorio Emanuelle II Monument 52

WALKS 59-84
Weather 94
Websites 105
What to Pack 98

THINGS CHANGE!

Phone numbers, prices, addresses, quality of food, etc, all change. If you come across any new information, we'd appreciate hearing from you. No item is too small! Drop us an email note at: Jopenroad@aol.com, or write us at:

Rome Made Easy
Open Road Publishing, P.O. Box 284
Cold Spring Harbor, NY 11724

TRAVEL NOTES

TRAVEL NOTES

TRAVEL NOTES

TRAVEL NOTES

OPEN ROAD PUBLISHING

Look for all of Open Road's *new* European travel and menu-reader guides:

- Paris Made Easy, $9.95
- London Made Easy, $9.95
- Rome Made Easy, $9.95
- Provence Made Easy, $9.95
- Amsterdam Made Easy, $9.95
- Berlin Made Easy, $9.95 (Fall 2005)
- Eating & Drinking in Paris, $9.95
- Eating & Drinking in Italy, $9.95
- Eating & Drinking in Spain, $9.95

For US orders, include $4.00 for postage and handling for the first book ordered; for each additional book, add $1.00. Orders outside US, inquire first about shipping charges (money order payable in US dollars on US banks only for overseas shipments). Send to:

Open Road Publishing
PO Box 284, Cold Spring Harbor, NY 11724

New European Guides